PIERS PLOWMAN
THE EVIDENCE FOR
AUTHORSHIP

PIERS PLOWMAN

THE EVIDENCE FOR AUTHORSHIP

BY

GEORGE KANE

UNIVERSITY OF LONDON
THE ATHLONE PRESS
1965

Published by
THE ATHLONE PRESS
UNIVERSITY OF LONDON
at 2 Gower Street, London WC1
Distributed by Constable & Co Ltd
12 Orange Street, London WC2

Canada
Oxford University Press
Toronto

U.S.A.
Oxford University Press Inc
New York

© *George Kane*, 1965

Printed in Great Britain by
WESTERN PRINTING SERVICES LTD
BRISTOL

PREFACE

IT WAS not part of the original plan of the Athlone Press edition of *Piers Plowman* to include discussion of the authorship of the poem. The editors were agreed in judging that no real case for multiple authorship had been made out. It appeared to us that in this we received authoritative support from a consensus of Middle English scholars. We were satisfied that the hypothesis of single authorship was the best hypothesis to account for all aspects of the relation between the three versions of the poem. To occupy ourselves with a vexed question which, in our view, should never have been raised, seemed an unprofitable distraction from the immediate, major problem of textual criticism. But as the first page of the following essay indicates, I succumbed to the distraction; more precisely, it forced itself on me as a study which I could not defer. And it has turned out to be not unprofitable. For the positive character of the result, which at the outset nothing in the history of the subject led me to expect, has materially reduced the hypothetical element in our editorial position. This change has seemed important enough to warrant the formal association of the essay which presents my findings with the edition as a supplementary volume.

Most of my particular obligations for details of information and for expert opinion are acknowledged in the body of the essay. For extensive, more general help, I am gravely in debt: to Professors Norman Davis and J. A. W. Bennett for reading the essay in typescript and much improving it by criticism and suggestions; to Professor George Russell for information about the C version which he is editing; above all to my co-editor of B, Professor Talbot Donaldson, for advice and encouragement no less than for his genial acquiescence in my truancy from our joint undertaking. I would add my thanks to the Board of Trinity College, Dublin and the Trustees of the Huntington Library for permission to publish facsimiles of parts of the *Piers Plowman* manuscripts in their care.

Royal Holloway College
Englefield Green   G.K.

CONTENTS

PLATES

I

THE RATIONALE OF ASCRIPTION

The question whether one or several poets wrote the three forms of the poem which we call *Piers Plowman* has been renewed by the appearance of a book[1] comparing the **A** and **B** versions in the belief that they were not written by the same man. Its author, describing himself as 'a member of the multiple authorship "school" ',[2] implies not only that the issue of single or multiple authorship is still open, but also that either position is at least as reasonably held as the opposed one. His first implication must be allowed, since his book is one more move in the old controversy and thus keeps it in being; it is immaterial in that connexion how small the 'school' to which he adheres may be. His second implication does not, however, seem so readily acceptable, since a point not of critical opinion or faith but of historical fact is at issue, and there can be only one truth with respect to it. The argument for multiple authorship of the *Piers Plowman* poems is that on internal evidence they cannot have been written by a single man; therefore the external evidence which ascribes *Piers Plowman* to William Langland is false, or has been incorrectly understood. The case for single authorship in the controversy was that no internal evidence against single authorship exists, and indeed that internal evidence argues strongly for single authorship, supporting the ascription. This continued opposition is intolerable: there should, in principle, be a reasonable, a correct way of interpreting the whole body of evidence, one that will provide an unambiguous answer, final at least in the present state of knowledge. If correctly assessed this evidence should point to a single truth, and that it has not done so implies, for me at least, that the assessment has been faulty. The *Piers Plowman* poems were composed by one man or by several: only one of these alternatives can be true. There is some evidence;

[1] D. C. Fowler, *Piers the Plowman: Literary Relations of the A and B Texts*, Seattle, 1961.
[2] p. ix.

it must embody a necessary conclusion, and the truth should be attainable by right thinking.

A fresh study of the literature of the controversy[1] has convinced me that the overriding reason why it reached no conclusion is the fact that it took the form of a debate, a notoriously unreliable means of ascertaining the truth because it can imply firmly adopted positions that cannot be surrendered without loss of face, and puts a premium on skill of advocacy rather than judiciousness. The main activity of a debate, that is scoring points off the opposition, or making brilliant rebuttals, can affect its issue in details only. Partisanship and passion or loyalties may cloud judgement: then contrary evidence is ignored or belittled; *ex parte* arguments are employed; situations are misrepresented; the terminology begs the question; misleading considerations are raised; the real issue disappears from view. All this took place in the controversy. But, regrettably, to insist on its inefficiency is not to undo its effects. By its occurrence it has permanently shaped the problem of the authorship of *Piers Plowman* for those to whom, at a later date, this is a matter of concern. The truth, now, will be determined only by re-establishing the real issue, that is by making and maintaining the distinction of principle and practice which was notably absent from the disputation: a distinction between the two main classes of evidence in question, internal and external,[2] and their correct employment. An assessment is called for of the relative validity of external evidence on the one hand, and of allegedly contrary internal evidence on the other. Even if belief in single authorship

[1] Summarized to 1936 by M. W. Bloomfield in 'The Present State of *Piers Plowman* Studies', *Speculum*, xiv (1939), pp. 215–32. The discussion is continued in: R. W. Chambers, 'Incoherencies in the A- and B-Texts of *Piers Plowman* and their Bearing on the Authorship', *London Mediæval Studies*, i (1937), pp. 27–39; R. W. Chambers, 'Robert or William Longland?' *London Mediæval Studies*, i (1948 for 1939), pp. 430–62; B. F. Huppé, 'The Authorship of the A and B Texts of *Piers Plowman*', *Speculum*, xxii (1947), pp. 578–620; J. R. Hulbert, '*Piers the Plowman* after Forty Years', *MP*, xlv (1947–8), pp. 215–25; T. Stroud, 'Manly's Marginal Notes on the "Piers Plowman" Controversy', *MLN*, lxiv (1949), pp. 9–12; E. T. Donaldson, *Piers Plowman: The C-Text and Its Poet*, New Haven, 1949; H. Meroney, 'The Life and Death of Longe Wille', *ELH*, xvii (1950), pp. 1–35; E. St John Brooks, 'The *Piers Plowman* Manuscripts in Trinity College, Dublin', *The Library*, fifth series, vi (1951), pp. 141–53; D. C. Fowler, 'The Relationship of the Three Texts of *Piers the Plowman*', *MP*, l (1952–3), pp. 5–22; E. T. Donaldson, 'The Texts of *Piers Plowman*: Scribes and Poets', *MP*, ˙(1952–3), pp. 269–73; A. G. Mitchell and G. H. Russell, 'The Three Texts of "Piers the Plowman"', *JEGP*, lii (1953), pp. 445–56.

[2] It has been convenient and (I think) profitable to identify a third class of evidence, that of literary history. Discussion of this takes place in IV, pp. 52ff. below.

were today unanimous such an assessment would still be due. I propose to attempt it here, not in the hope of converting Professor Fowler, though that would indeed be a gratifying achievement, but with the primary intention of working out to the best of my powers the true force of the arguments on both sides.

The assessment must be preceded by some clarification of issues. The first has to do with the state of the text of the poem. It used often to be said[1] that the question of authorship would never be finally settled until 'critical' texts of the three versions were available; when the true readings had been 'scientifically' determined considerations of dialect, vocabulary, alliteration, etc. might well be decisive. That this prospect was illusory must be stated without delay. For one thing, as will nowadays be realized, even the most 'scientific' editing will be unlikely ever to recover the original linguistic form of this poem. For another, as will appear on reflection, it must be quite impossible for an 'impartial' editor of *Piers Plowman*, that is one who reserves judgement about the authorship question, to make any real progress beyond the restoration of the archetypal text of a version. Unless he will commit himself about authorship he can barely proceed; and if he adopts a position this will radically affect his editorial decisions. Towards the solution of the authorship problem we have now as much help from the minutiae of the texts as we are ever likely to have, and that is precious little. Moreover editing and the establishment of authorship are distinct processes. What the editor of *Piers Plowman* does when he edits is to create, out of textual detail, a hypothesis of original readings based ultimately on an assumption (however well or ill founded) about authorship. If his hypothetical structure is satisfactory in the light of what is known about the transmission of Middle English texts that is all to the good, but it is no proof of his assumption about authorship, for it rests upon this assumption. To invoke his success as such proof would be to argue in a circle. Since, then, no single reconstructed text, and *a fortiori* no individual manuscripts can properly be used for argument in detail about authorship, the matter must be settled without recourse to such considerations.

[1] Most recently by Hulbert, p. 218, but cp. also Γ. Λ. Knott, 'Observations on the Authorship of "Piers the Plowman"' II, *MP*, xv (1917–18), p. 41.

Similarly the reconstruction of a biography of the poet from indications in the texts of the three versions will not be considered as proof of authorship in the assessment. Such biographical argument was a feature of the advocacy of single authorship. Ingenuity and resource as well as wise insight into the possibilities of the growth of a poet's mind distinguished the reconstructions, and it may well be that in many particulars their inferences were correct. But viewed strictly in their setting of controversy the essays in biographical detection were no more than declarations of faith: 'I believe in single authorship because I can perceive a single personality and the unfolding of one man's artistic and spiritual career in the successive forms and content of this poetry.' As proofs of single authorship they fell short in several ways. First, they required an assumption that the autobiography of Will the Dreamer suggested in the poems necessarily corresponded in some considerable degree to that of the actual poet. And whether such an assumption is correct or not,[1] its necessity with respect to any particular detail can be challenged. Second, viewed logically they were simply demonstrations that if single authorship of the poems is assumed a plausible biographical hypothesis can be constructed from their texts. How distinct this is from proof of single authorship appears on consideration of its converse implication: that when a hypothetical biography cannot be reconstructed from the content of a corpus of poetry, then that poetry cannot have been written by a single man.[2]

The appeal of the argument from biography was to the imagination and sensibility;[3] beyond consuming effort and swelling the bulk of the literature of the subject it probably did no great harm, and its findings may yet, if the question of authorship can be

---

[1] The assumption, as will appear in IV below, receives a kind of general encouragement from literary history. But it cannot be absolutely maintained, and if it is made with qualification it has no real force as an argument for single authorship.

[2] Both sides were sometimes remarkably naïve in their approach to the question of autobiography. Compare Hulbert's 'it is not credible that the conscientious author of A fell victim to the sins of the flesh after writing A' (p. 221). It would be comforting to think that to have composed 2,500 lines of moral poetry might be a safeguard against human frailty. Hulbert should have remembered the tendency to exaggerate which is a frequent element in public confession.

[3] It has not been without effect, answering the need which the *Piers Plowman* poetry creates in many readers for the realization of a personality behind it. So Hulbert perceived (p. 215). He neglected to observe that an appeal of comparable force is exercised on certain

settled, come into their own. But a really pernicious consideration, seriously advanced as an appeal to logic, was that of the 'burden of proof'. The most strenuous exponent of this was probably Moore,[1] but both sides made play with it, especially after winning a point in the debate, and its invocation probably reflects the various controversialists' uneasy sense of the difference between rebuttal and the presentation of evidence.[2] The contention that a burden of proof exists implies opposition, irrevocably adopted positions, minds already closed, a concern with winning the case rather than discovering the truth. A product of controversy, it is extraneous and intrusive, having no rightful place in a dispassionate scrutiny of evidence. Its forensic nature must be an obstacle to the attainment of the truth; it was probably the worst feature of the disputatious conduct of the proceedings.

We are left, then, with the essential problem: a situation in which it is contended that external and internal evidence about the author-ship of the three versions of *Piers Plowman* are at variance. The starting point must be that the two classes of evidence differ radi-cally in their nature. From this fact arise considerations which, though they may seem elementary and indeed obvious, are never-theless fundamental.

In a case of ascription the character of external evidence is that it exists absolutely, in some determinable way independent of the text which it concerns. It may be bad; its accuracy can be questioned, but its existence cannot. It is a kind of physical fact. Internal evidence, by contrast, is a critical postulate. It has a contingent character, depending for its existence on being identified as such by someone, and for its validity upon, first, the correctness of the identification, and second, the quality of the reasoning applied to it. Thus by their nature the two classes of evidence are subject to

mentalities by iconoclastic or destructive criticism, or alternately by the notion of being associated with a novel proposition, especially if acceptance of this is made to seem a mark of enlightenment. There is also the circumstance that the theory of multiple authorship was one of the first really sensational proposals of Middle English scholarship, giving this a status similar to classical and biblical studies at a time when destructive criticism was strong in those fields.

[1] S. Moore, 'Studies in *Piers the Plowman*' I, *MP*, xi (1913–14), pp. 177ff.; ibid. II, *MP*, xii (1914–15), pp. 19–25.

[2] To cry 'the burden of proof lies with you' was a kind of triumphant challenge to the opposition to try again—with the implication that the fresh attempt would be hopeless.

different assessments. For external evidence, apart from the need to understand its literal meaning, the test is whether it is historically true or false. With respect to internal evidence there are, meanwhile, two doubtful factors: whether, first, its identification as a feature of the text is correct, that is whether it actually exists; and, second, whether the inferences drawn from it are logically compelling, that is, the necessary or the most probable inferences.

Although from this description external evidence might seem essentially superior to the internal kind, the latter is nevertheless to be taken seriously. As students of literature we are often obliged to work with it, and there have been enough cases where its testimony has been allowed in the face of contrary external evidence. It has been proclaimed that we have here such an opposition. The ques/ tion then is what means there are for testing the two classes of evidence: whether the external evidence is truthful and what it means; whether the internal evidence genuinely exists, and what inferences from it are logically authorized.

With external evidence it is the quality, not the fact of existence, which is in question. Notwithstanding its objective existence, it may obviously be partly or wholly false. It may contain erroneous information, set down in good faith but in entire or partial ignor/ ance of the real facts, from an ill/informed source, or from wrong inference, or from faulty memory. It may be a deliberate mis/ statement, designed to conceal the truth and to mislead. The tests which apply are those of the historian. Is it genuine, that is physic/ ally authentic, or a modern forgery? Is it knowledgeable? How old is it? Is the source of its content ascertainable? Is the person re/ sponsible for it likely to have had access to the kind of information which it contains? Is its honesty presumable; or inferable? Can motives for its being a falsification be discovered or reasonably conjectured? The answers to these questions will determine its authority as evidence. Further, is it verifiable in all or any particulars? If contrary external evidence exists, is this of equal, or greater or less authority? External evidence can be misinterpreted. What, in the terms of its time, does it mean?

The two distinct factors of doubt in internal evidence are to be tested in different ways. First, whether the identification of the feature of the text which is held to constitute the evidence is correct:

this depends on its exponent's sensibility and perceptivity, and will be tested by the exercise of corresponding faculties in his readers. So far the matter is subjective. But other considerations also, of intelligent scholarly practice, must apply. Is the identification based on a correct reading of the text? Does it take account of the whole text, or select appropriate elements only? Is it informed with respect to external data bearing on the subject matter? Does it show understanding of the nature and processes of poetry? In general does it impress as critically sound, surviving impartial scrutiny and the passage of time? Supposing the identification to fulfil all these requirements, the second test is of the quality of the reasoning by which conclusions are derived from it. This is a matter of the most elementary logic, indeed of simple common sense. Are the inferences drawn from the feature of the text the necessary, or at least the most probable ones? Or do other inferences seem equally possible? Are the assumptions underlying the inferences easy and acceptable, or difficult, or even evidently convenient to the argument, that is evidently *ex parte*? If a hypothesis is constructed, is it the best possible one, having the broadest basis of fact, the fewest hard assumptions, and the least element of conjecture? The test of internal evidence is thus partly subjective, conducted by the reader's own response, partly a matter of intelligence and fact, and partly logical. Its processes correspond to those by which internal evidence is identified and interpreted. Every sensitive, percipient, informed and alert reading of an argument from internal evidence can thus amount to a test of it.[1]

All these considerations bear upon the centre of the authorship problem, which is the alleged opposition between the two classes of evidence. There is a note in a manuscript of *Piers Plowman* which records that a *willielmus de langlond* '*fecit librum qui vocatur Perys ploughman*'.[2] But arguments are advanced from the texts of the three *Piers Plowman* poems that these cannot possibly have been written by one man. They must, therefore, be something else than successive

---

[1] From this the value of a consensus of judgement over a period of time may be apparent. Thus in the *Piers Plowman* controversy the willingness of the majority of the interested public to let the discussion subside and accept single authorship for practical purposes might be held to constitute a rejection of the arguments against it from internal evidence. But I do not press this.

[2] Discussed at length, pp. 26ff. below.

versions of a single poem; therefore, also, not all can be by William Langland; and the note is wrong or has been misunderstood.

The character of this opposition directs attention first to the internal evidence advanced against single authorship. What matters, in the critical sense, is not who wrote these poems but whether one man wrote them; whether they are to be seen as successive attempts by the same poet to realize an artistic conception, or whether they are three separate works of art. This is the main historical fact at issue. Who, in either instance, wrote them, is less directly material. Therefore I begin with an assessment of the arguments against single authorship. Are they critically, logically and historically compelling? If they prove so to be, the note ascribing *Piers Plowman* to Langland can be disregarded as referring at best to some one of the versions; if not it must be re-examined, since the possibility of its truthfulness has not been excluded.

II

INTERNAL EVIDENCE

The assessment of the internal evidence advanced against single authorship will not take the form of a summary of the controversy. My intention is not to answer arguments but to test them, and this would be hampered by reproducing the give and take of disputation and by the accompanying commitment to interpretation. From the wordy and extended wrangles about detail a number of chief arguments stand out. These[1] will now receive attention.

The principal argument against single authorship, singled out by Knott,[2] has been that the **A** and **B** versions of *Piers Plowman* differ so much in language, versification, number and kind of rhetorical devices, structure and organization, as well as in the mental and poetic capacities, psychological characteristics, interests and views which they exhibit, that they and consequently the **C** version as well cannot be the work of a single man.[3] The question is then whether such differences have been correctly identified, and whether they necessarily or probably rule out the possibility of single authorship. The several kinds require separate consideration.

I begin with the differences in language, dialect, sentence

---

[1] They are identified in the following publications, where the essential case against single authorship is made out: J. M. Manly, 'The Lost Leaf of "Piers the Plowman"', *MP*, iii (1905–6), pp. 359–66, repr. in EETS OS Extra Volume, 135B (1908), pp. viii–xiv (when citing this and the two immediately following items I use the page numbers of the 1910 EETS Collection *The Piers Plowman Controversy*, comprising OS issues 135B (1908) and 139b–e (1910)); J. M. Manly, '*Piers the Plowman* and its Sequence', *CHEL*, ii, ch. i, repr. in EETS OS Extra Volume 135B (1908), pp. 1–42; J. M. Manly, 'The Authorship of *Piers Plowman*', *MP*, vii (1909–10), pp. 83–144, repr. in EETS OS Extra Issue, 139c (1910), pp. 1–62; S. Moore, 'Studies in *Piers the Plowman*' I, *MP*, xi (1913–14), pp. 177–93; ibid. II, *MP*, xii (1914–15), pp. 19–50; T. A. Knott, 'Observations on the Authorship of "Piers the Plowman"' I, *MP*, xiv (1916–17), pp. 531–58; ibid. II, *MP*, xv (1917–18), pp. 23–41; M. Day, 'The Revisions of "Piers Plowman"', *MLR*, xxiii (1928), pp. 1–27; T. P. Dunning, *Piers Plowman: An Interpretation of the A-Text*, Dublin, 1937, esp. pp. 194ff.; J. R. Hulbert, passim.

[2] 'Observations' I, pp. 532–3.

[3] See Manly, 'The Lost Leaf', p. viii; '*Piers the Plowman* and its Sequence', pp. 4, 17, 18, 24; Knott, 'Observations' I, pp. 532–3; Day, 'The Revisions', passim; Dunning, pp. 194ff.; Hulbert, pp. 217, 218, 221, 222.

9

structure, versification and figures of speech. The position with respect to these has already been indicated (p. 3 above): they are excluded from use as evidence for authorship because of the textual situation. The original dialect of the poems is not determinable; recovery of the original vocabulary, and even the original forms of many lines (where tropes are concerned) can be attempted only after making an assumption about authorship. Without such an assumption the limit of editorial possibility is the recovery of the exclusive common ancestor or archetype of the surviving manu‐ scripts of each version. There is no way of knowing how far such an archetype preserves the linguistic character of the original manuscripts, and there is more than a possibility (from the known character of scribal transmission) that it may not reproduce the original words of the text at any given point. It seems clear, then, that arguments from detailed differences between the various forms of the poem can have no force, since the differences are not identifi‐ able as necessarily originating with the poet or poets.

Next to be considered are the differences in psychological characteristics, interests and views allegedly observable in the *Piers Plowman* poems. In so far as argument from such differences takes the form of reconstructing the creative identities of distinct poets it is subject to the same strictures as apply to the argument from bio‐ graphy (above, p. 4). The 'psychological characteristics' referred to in Knott's summary of this class of evidence[1] would come under this head, but I find them nowhere specified. If, however, the differences in 'psychological characteristics' are understood as differences of poetic and imaginative response to a diversity of topics their identification and use in argument must be examined.

First with respect to the identification of the internal evidence. Certainly the *Piers Plowman* poems exhibit a very broad range of interest in moral, social and theological topics. But it now seems very doubtful whether this breadth of interest has the significance claimed for it, and whether it is identifiable with differences of interest in the controversial sense. For as Hulbert pointed out[2] it has been shown[3] that the various themes of *Piers Plowman* belong to a

---

[1] 'Observations' I, p. 532. [2] p. 216.
[3] By G. R. Owst, *Literature and Pulpit in Medieval England*, Cambridge, 1933. See Index s.v. *Langland*.

large body of related material which constitutes a single, embracing interest; also it appears that the differing views on various elements in this body of material are not radically opposed. If Owst is substantially correct the sum of attitudes to the various topics or 'interests', the 'tone of thought' in *Piers Plowman,* is 'in perfect accord with that of the most commonplace orthodox preaching of the times'.[1] Thus it seems that the identification of internal evidence here was made in ignorance, and this, while pardonable to be sure,[2] must invalidate it.

Because, however, the argument from differences of views and interests is still being applied as evidence against single authorship,[3] the manner of its use requires to be examined. The underlying form of reasoning seems to be as follows. When several parts of a body of poetry on associated topics exhibit differences of interest and differences of opinion, those interests and views are necessarily exclusive of one another, in the sense that the several parts cannot be imputed to a single author. Differences of interest and views are discernible in the various *Piers Plowman* poems. Therefore these poems must be by several authors. The dubious quality of the second proposition has already been shown in the preceding paragraph; the first is also unacceptable because, by failing to take account of the effects of time on a poet, it defies the known facts of literary history. This will be seen from the assumption, variously expressible, which it implies: that a poet's preoccupations at one moment of composition will be lifelong preoccupations; *or* that a poet's sense of the relative importance of the issues of his time will be constant; *or* that a poet, throughout his career, will respond to one particular class of experience only; *or* that a poet will be unaffected by experience, even the experience of having written a particular kind of poem; *or* that a poet's opinions on all or any subjects are unlikely to change. Such an assumption, however expressed, is clearly unjustified. For the argument from differences of interest and views to be at all compelling the possibility of the poet's development, and that not necessarily always or in all respects for the better, would have to be excluded. The opponents of single authorship did

---

[1] *Literature and Pulpit,* p. 548. He is quoted by Hulbert.

[2] Since Owst's book had not yet appeared.

[3] Fowler's book (see above, p. 1) appears to be wholly based on the assumption that such differences exist.

not, of course, miss the need for this exclusion but I do not find that they ever faced its logical implications squarely. Manly, when he asserted that the differences seemed to him 'of such a nature as not to admit of such an explanation' (that is by reference to a single poet's development), was simply modifying the first proposition of the argument sketched above by including in it considerations of the degree or kind of difference. In doing so he made the argument turn on his subjective judgement; subsequent scholarship[1] appears to have discredited that judgement as exercised in ignorance. Thus in- ferences about multiple authorship from differences of interests and views seem not to be necessary inferences; they are challenged by contrary inferences based on the possibility of change or develop- ment in a single poet; and the assessment of probability by those arguing against single authorship is made on subjective grounds which are far from compelling.

Next to be considered is the argument from specifically literary differences between the several forms of *Piers Plowman*. Of these it was maintained that they were such as could not occur within the corpus of a single poet: they must necessarily reflect the activities of several poets of distinctive mental powers and poetic capabilities. Two specific differences between A^1 and the remaining *Piers Plowman* poetry, of organization, and of visual effect, formed the particular issue.[2]

There are undoubtedly differences, both of effect and of structure, in the several forms of *Piers Plowman*. They could be minimized or their existence denied only in the heat of disputation, just as that same contentious fervour could result in their exaggeration or misrepresentation, or muddy the logic of inferences drawn from them.

In assessing the accuracy of the judgement by which the differ- ences are identified we re-enact it, employing our own critical faculty. Mine tells me that, with respect to the superiority of **A**, and to **B** 'spoiling' **A**, the case against single authorship rests generally on exaggeration and particularly on selective treatment of **B**, that is on critical judgements not equally applicable to all parts of **B**. Meanwhile the two poems certainly differ. One is in large part clear, simple, highly organized, graphic; the other digressive,

[1] That of Owst referred to above.   [2] They are singled out by Hulbert, p. 217.

speculative, sometimes abstract, often obscure, of uneven artistic quality. But notwithstanding this broad general difference the criticism which makes **B** out to be always or uniformly the inferior in organization and visual effect leaves many passages of **B** out of account; the criticism which asserts the poor quality of **B**'s confession of Wrath is shockingly *ex parte*;[1] there is (for me at least) no height of achievement in **A** to match the sublimity of parts of **B** XVIII. One poem is generally better organized and has a more consistently visual effect than the other. To that extent only the identification of differences of organization and effect was accurate. With respect to particulars it was more often than not of dubious accuracy.

With respect to the logic of inference, for a start the differences in question could be made to serve the case of multiple authorship only by *petitio principii*. There are, for the purpose of this argument, two *Piers Plowman* poems, **A** and **B**. Of these the former is found to be superior in some literary respects to the latter. But not uniformly so: **A** IX–XI in many ways resemble **B** more than they resemble **A** Prologue–VIII. That fact is inconvenient to the argument, for if **A** Prologue–XI are treated as a unity the differences in question between **A** and **B** appear less marked, since **A** Prologue–XI are uneven in quality and effect. To turn the differences to controversial advantage they must be isolated; this is accomplished by begging the question of the part and the whole as follows. Although **A** is established by manuscript tradition as a physical unity it cannot be an artistic unity because there is a difference of literary quality between its first and second parts. Since it cannot be an artistic unity it cannot be by a single poet. Therefore its two parts are in fact two separate poems. And since this is so the quality of **A**[1], an artistic unity, reflecting the mental powers and poetic capabilities of a single poet, may be employed in comparison, as exclusively representative, to test the authorship of **A**[2] and **B**.

There are of course circumstances in which inferences from literary quality and effects can be applied with good logic to the question of authorship. Where a sufficiently large body of writings known beyond doubt to be by a particular author exists, its characteristics provide a sum of critical information by which the

[1] Manly, 'The Lost Leaf', p. xiii.

ascription or rejection of other writings can be carried out. But where there is not such undisputed information available, what are to be the delimitations? How is a beginning to be made? The difficulty, in the case of *Piers Plowman*, is shown by representing the assumption required before the evidence of different quality and effects can be used in argument against single authorship.

This assumption can, again, be variously expressed: that a single poet will not write in various ways and with varying success at different times in his life; *or* that a poet, rehandling similar or associated material at successive times is bound by his first handling as by a self-imposed prescription; *or* that if **B** were by the author of **A**, then this man would necessarily continue with **B** as he had begun in **A**,[1] his revision being necessarily designed to produce a larger poem along the lines of **A**. This assumption, however phrased, seems to me neither sound nor easy, and the facts of literary history as I know them do not encourage me to accept it, any more than they convince me that the revisions of poets are necessarily for the better, or necessarily increasingly successful. Meanwhile the possibility of revision by a single author, necessarily implying dissatisfaction with a first effort, or a sense of the possibility of improving this, or a change or growth of imaginative conception, would afford grounds for a contrary assumption at least as compelling, to make only the minimal claim for it. For I do not see how it can be accepted that if the three (or four[2]) *Piers Plowman* poems are by a single author they must, as a man's life work, constitute an artistic whole, for it seems to me that the utmost permissible critical requirement is that there should be evident a striving for unity of conception within the single poem. Nor can the assumption be improved by introducing into it considerations of the extreme degree of the differences involved; it remains difficult notwithstanding, for the extremity of the differences is questionable, being once more a matter of subjective estimation.

Finally has this comparison of literary quality been carried out according to good critical practice? First with respect to the internal organization of **B**. Even if we discount exaggeration such as

---

[1] So Hulbert (p. 223) assumes: 'If there was to be [a continuation], we should have expected an extension which would not be at all like the B text.'

[2] Taking into account the division into A^1 and A^2.

Manly's assertion that the poet of **B** was 'at the mercy of any chance association of words and ideas',[1] the comparison seems critically injudicious. For it leaves quite out of account the fact that one kind of undertaking can be easier than another, and can offer greater chances of success. The problem of organization when composing a relatively circumscribed moral and social allegory is one thing; the economy of an extended, speculative, often allegorical, sometimes symbolical representation of a multiplicity of doctrinal and spiritual topics conceived in terms of their contemporary application appears a harder undertaking. It does not seem as if a critic would be justified in postulating that a single poet, successively attempting these two undertakings, must adopt the same manner of proceeding in both, or accomplish both with equal success. Similarly the differences in the degree of visual effect[2] between, say **A**[1] and **B**, as far as they may be allowed, have not been subjected to sound criticism. Here a direct inference was made, from the existence of actual differences of visual effect in the poems to the existence of necessarily corresponding differences in ability to create visual effects, and thus to the existence of several poets, which left quite out of account the different visual potentialities of various kinds of subject matter, concrete and abstract. But it would seem more than possible, indeed likely, for the same poet writing of more concrete subjects to produce one effect, and of abstract or speculative subjects, another. Chaucer describing Alisoun and Chaucer conducting a discussion of predestination, the poet of **B** illustrating the nature of the Trinity or representing the Crucifixion, exhibit markedly different responses to their subjects. Meanwhile the confessions of the Sins in **A** V and Hawkin's account of his various frailties in **B** are not so very different in the degree of visual effect. The visual effects in any given part of any poet's work do not necessarily reflect his whole capacity to create visual effects.

With respect to critical accuracy, logic and conformity to the processes of literature, then, the argument that the differences of literary quality, in particular differences of organization and visual

[1] *CHEL*, ii, p. 24. The accuracy of this extreme contention is of course not determinable, since we know of only those distractions to which he apparently succumbed, but it seems *prima facie* unlikely.

[2] Manly, *CHEL*, ii, p. 32; Day, 'The Revisions', pp. 18ff. Hulbert (p. 217), reviewing the controversy, insists on the importance of this kind of difference.

effect, are necessarily evidence against the single authorship of *Piers Plowman* falls short of being compelling. It has not ruled out the contrary hypothesis: that an inspiration greater, more ambitious, more difficult to realize, developing out of a first relatively limited and accessible undertaking, could result in the poem of this successful first undertaking being incorporated (with some admitted detriment to its quality) into a larger, less perfectly realized whole.

The second main argument against single authorship relates to internal evidence which, it is held, indicates misunderstanding of **A** by the poet of **B**, or his imperfect familiarity with the content of **A**, the incomprehension and the unfamiliarity being such as could not have occurred if **A** and **B** were by the same poet.[1] The first proposition of an argument from such evidence must be that an author revising his own earlier work would first understand his original undertaking well enough to leave no traces of incomprehension (this, naturally, one would accept), and second be sufficiently familiar with it, as well as take sufficient pains, to fit new material without discrepancy ('incongruity') neatly into the existing substance. As the two branches refer to distinct conditions of the text they must be considered separately.

I begin with the argument that **B** misunderstands **A**. The proposition by which such misunderstanding becomes evidence against single authorship requires the assumption that the textual signs of a second poet's incomprehension of a first poet's work can be clearly and confidently distinguished from the textual signs of a single poet's radical change of artistic conception and intention. This may obviously sometimes be possible, but the assumption is not really so acceptable as might appear, especially when the text in question is not particularly easy. For the sure identification of incomprehension presumes a reader who perfectly understands both the passage not comprehended and the passage exhibiting incomprehension with respect, in both cases, to actual or achieved meaning; to intended meaning; and to the rôle of the passage in the design of the whole poem. Understanding the actual meaning depends on an accurate reading in all senses of that term, including

[1] See for instance Manly, 'The Lost Leaf', pp. viiiff.; *CHEL*, ii, pp. 32–34; 'The Authorship', pp. 19ff.; Knott, 'Observations' I, pp. 534ff.; II, pp. 23, 37, 40–41; Day, 'The Revisions', pp. 18ff.; Dunning, pp. 194ff.

the reader's possession of sufficient knowledge of the subject. Understanding the 'intended' meaning amounts to identifying the poet's intention, which is notoriously possible only by *a posteriori* rationalization. And since the possibility of single authorship has not been excluded, identification of incomprehension must assume that the relation of the texts in question cannot be better explained as the result of a single author's change of intention on rehandling his material.

The force of these considerations will appear from the great case in point: the argument for **B**'s incomprehension of **A** which was based on the absence of a confession of Wrath from **A** V and the character of the representation of Wrath in the corresponding part of **B**. It was argued that the revising poet of **B**, while he was aware from external knowledge of hamartiology that **A** must necessarily once have contained a confession of Wrath, and that this must therefore have been lost from his copy of **A**, displayed in his management of this passage spectacular ignorance of the meaning and original form of **A**, and supplied out of his own head an artistically inferior confession of Wrath quite inappropriate to the **A** context in which he set it. But it now appears that Manly's vehement insistence on the necessary original presence of a confession of Wrath in **A**[1] was the consequence of a multiple misreading. It postulated, from an impression of the symmetry of the confessions in **A** V which the text does not confirm[2] and from a mistaken

[1] 'The Lost Leaf', pp. xi–xii.

[2] This absence of symmetry in **A** V, which is more important to the argument than the controversialists allowed, can be quickly shown by summaries of the representations of the six personages. A proud woman (not *superbia*) prays for mercy, resolves to mortify her flesh, and to conduct herself henceforward in meek humility (9 lines). A lecherous man (not *luxuria*) calls on the Virgin to intercede for him, offering for his part an undertaking to avoid occasion of sin (4 lines). *Invidia* is described, behaves enviously, specifies the effect of envy and wrath upon himself, recounts sinful actions, regards his state as beyond remedy, and doubts the power of confession to effect this (45 lines). *Cupiditas* is described, confesses a career of dishonest trade by himself and his wife, and makes a resolution of amendment (39 lines). A gluttonous man (not *gula*) on the way to confession succumbs to temptation, embarks on a drinking bout, and when he finally wakes from the subsequent drunken stupor responds to rebuke, experiences contrition, and makes a resolution of amendment (67 lines). *Accidia*, overcome by *tristitia*, is saved from despair by an injunction to contrition and a reminder of divine mercy; then with a solemn vow he resolves to mend his ways (20 lines). Not one of these representations is planned like any other, and the longest is 16 times the length of the shortest. If a confession of Wrath was lost from **A**, there is little indication of its form and length in what has survived. (For a possible explanation of the disproportionate treatments see Dunning, pp. 81–84.)

17

belief that the number of Deadly Sins in such a representation would invariably be seven,[1] the physical loss of a confession of Wrath from **A**. This postulate may have involved a misconception of the poet's intention in his representation of the Sins;[2] certainly the further argument that the representation of Wrath found in **B** was inappropriate to the other treatments (leaving aside the questionable character of this judgement, or the argument that the changes made in this passus by **C** necessarily relate to a third author) rested on the assumption that the original poet, rehandling this passage, could not experience a change of intention. The argument constituted, moreover, a classic example of *petitio principii* as follows. The **A** version as a whole shows its poet to have been a careful artist. Therefore the text of **A** V as it stands cannot re-present the work of this poet in its true form.[3] Thus Manly's prejudgement of the necessary presence of a confession of Wrath in **A**, with its two assumptions, that the quality of organization in a poem will be uniform and that in this case the presentation would necessarily be congruent with a complete and systematic external scheme, failed to demonstrate incomprehension of **A** by the poet of **B**. The only incomprehension revealed was, indeed, incomprehen-sion of **A** by Manly.[4]

Now for the argument that **B** was imperfectly familiar with **A**, and as a result, by his additions, omissions and modifications, created discrepancies, 'incongruities', of various kinds such as would be inconceivable if he himself had written **A**.

[1] See M. W. Bloomfield, *The Seven Deadly Sins*, Michigan, 1952, esp. pp. 424-5, note 299.

[2] See Dunning, pp. 81-83, 195; it should, however, be noted that Bloomfield (op. et loc. cit.) disagrees with his inference of intention on grounds of external information.

[3] This is, of course, an argument similar to that applied by editors in the reconstruction of texts. The difference lies in the scale of its application, the amount of unquestioned information available, and the order of textual deficiency inferred from it. The impropriety of applying it to a question of ascription should be evident.

[4] Knott's fine reconstruction of the loss from A ('Observations' I, pp. 536-7) is then super-fluous. This hypothetical reconstruction, as a basis of argument, is, moreover, palæo-graphically by no means compelling. The 'lost leaf' (*sc.* lost fold) with its four sides of 30 lines each might have contained, on the one half, 59 lines corresponding to **B** V 129-87 (a few more lines on Envy followed by the confession of Wrath), and on the other, 58 lines corresponding to **B** V 392-449 (Sloth's account of his various sins), just as likely as it might have contained superior poetry on Wrath and Sloth by **A**. If there were convincing literary or doctrinal reasons for accepting the necessity of loss, then as a textual critic I should prefer this identification of the lost material to Knott's. But I do not believe that loss occurred here. (**B** references throughout are to W. W. Skeat, *The Vision of William concerning Piers the Plow-man*, ii, *Text B*, EETS 38, London, 1869.)

The first test must be whether, as internal evidence, the alleged discrepancies are in fact genuine. They cannot, obviously, all be examined here; it will be enough to show the importance of the test. A useful instance to begin with is the most famous and fought over: the alleged inappropriateness of **B** V 463–8 to Sloth. According to Manly these lines are 'entirely out of harmony with his character, and could never have been assigned to him by so careful an artist as **A**';[1] their application to Sloth in **B** must be the result of a second poet's bungling ignorance of **A**. The confidence with which the opponents of single authorship identified this discrepancy and proclaimed the necessity of their inference from it is notable, but appears to have been ill-founded, and the discrepancy may be non-existent.[2] Another, simpler instance is **B**'s addition of a confession of swearing to Glutton's representation (V 375–7). This was held to be inappropriate to Glutton.[3] But the collocation of *Glotonye & grete opes* in **A** II 64 (line 67 in Skeat[4]), associated as sins of the tongue in the **A** poet's mind, removes the ground for imputing their association in **B** V to a second poet; in any event the two sins are connected in hamartiology.[5] Another alleged discrepancy, the marriage of Meed to her father in **B** (II 25, 40)[6] is identifiable as necessarily discrepant only by the rigorous exclusion of meaning. To make the exclusion may be right, but how shall we know? Spenser in *An Hymne in Honour of Love* (ll. 52–53) gives Love three parents. Is that a discrepancy too? Yet another alleged discrepancy, Piers's changes in symbolic value,[7] appears such only by the exercise of unusual literal-mindedness; symbols are by their nature shifting conceptions, with respect to which we can scarcely exact from a single author consistency of meaning. These examples should sufficiently indicate the need for a cautious attitude towards the argument from discrepancies at its first

---

[1] 'The Lost Leaf', p. x. See also Knott, 'Observations' I, pp. 536, 538ff.

[2] This is the opinion of the ablest professional theologian yet to have concerned himself with *Piers Plowman*, reached at a time when he was a believer in multiple authorship. See Dunning, pp. 84–85.

[3] Dunning, p. 196.

[4] W. W. Skeat, *The Vision of William concerning Piers Plowman*, i, *Text A*, EETS 28, London, 1867. Unless otherwise specified, **A** references are to *Piers Plowman: The A Version*, ed. G. Kane, London, 1960.

[5] Bloomfield, *Seven Deadly Sins*, pp. 163, 168, and 425, n. 302.

[6] Day, 'The Revisions', p. 20. [7] Day, 'The Revisions', pp. 20, 22ff.

stage, which is their identification. That too calls for an accurate, informed and perceptive reading of the text.

Meanwhile, allowing that discrepancies, 'incongruities', were created in **B** and **C** by addition, omission or modification, what is the character of the argument by which they are presented as necessarily evidence against single authorship?

The first proposition of such an argument must necessarily be that when a single author revises his own earlier work he will always achieve a perfect assimilation of the old material and the new, and will never, in the course of his additions, omissions and modifica, tions, bring into existence and then through oversight or a new pre, occupation let stand discrepancies of any kind. In other words any revision of a poem by its original poet will be totally efficient and successful. This proposition, implying further that a poetic con, ception, of whatever magnitude, is perfectly realizable, cannot, of course, be accepted. That even the greatest poets have not always been in perfect control of their matter is a manifest fact; that poets who undertake long poems of complex organization can come to grief over detail is a truism of literature.[1]

The argument from discrepancies against single authorship depends, moreover, on the postulate that the three forms of *Piers Plowman* are perfected poems, 'published' in the modern sense, 'passed' by their poets as nowadays an author passes a 'revise' of a page proof. But this postulate, leaving aside its historical difficulty,[2] can be allowed only if their separate authorship is accepted. For if they are by one author the very fact of revision argues the unfinished, necessarily imperfect character of any version, except, in theory, the latest, if only because the act of revision implies dissatisfaction with the results of previous effort and therefore, presumably at least, ground for dissatisfaction. But their separate authorship has not yet been established; it is the matter at issue. Again the question is

[1] Classic instances are *The Faerie Queene* and *Paradise Lost*. See for example: J. H. Walter, '"The Faerie Queene": Alterations and Structure', *MLR*, xxxvi (1941), pp. 37–47; J. W. Bennett, *The Evolution of "The Faerie Queene"*, Chicago, 1942, esp. pp. 35–37; 42–43; 58, 94, 101, 132–3, 144–50, 165–6, 171–2, 174, 181, 184; A. H. Gilbert, *On the Composition of Paradise Lost*, Chapel Hill, 1947, esp. pp. 5, 49, 82–83, 96, 122, 125–6, 133–5, 136–50; J. B. Broadbent, *Some Graver Subject*, London, 1960, pp. 147–8.

[2] On this point see for example H. S. Bennett, 'The Production and Dissemination of Vernacular Manuscripts in the Fifteenth Century', *The Library*, fifth series, i (1947), pp. 167–78.

begged: evidence which could have force only after acceptance of the proposition under proof is offered as proof of that proposition. Until the possibility of single authorship has been excluded by other arguments discrepancies within the successive forms of *Piers Plowman* are susceptible of another explanation than separate authorship: that of imperfect assimilation by a single author, for whatever reason.

It is, further, worth observing that this postulate of the 'finished' character of these poems can be held, with respect to **A**, only in the face of strong contrary evidence. The critical opinion that **A** 'is a complete poem, admirably proportioned and clear in development'[1] is for a start debatable. As to **A**'s proportions it might well seem to some that the *Vita*, with its enormous doctrinal and spiritual implications, is sketchily developed by comparison with the *Visio*. Manly's conviction that **A** was by two authors[2] comes to mind; and there is before me Fowler's categorical assertion that 'the A-version of *Piers the Plowman* actually consists of two poems'.[3] Hulbert noted that in this clearly developed poem Will the Dreamer falls asleep in **A** IX 58 and is not reawakened by the poet.[4] Moore observed that while the incipit of **A** IX promises a development *secundum witte and Resoun*, Reason 'is not even mentioned in **A**[2]'; from this he very properly concluded that the author did not, in **A** IX–XI, 'execute all that he had planned of *Dowel, Dobet,* and *Dobest*'.[5] The failure to reawaken the Dreamer, and the unfulfilled promise to consult Reason[6] are strong evidence that **A** is an unfinished, or hastily concluded poem. One more piece of evidence to that effect is available in this same incipit for **A** IX, in the six complete, unmixed and rubricated **A** manuscripts, ADJMRU.[7] These manuscripts head Passus IX *Hic incipit vita de dowel dobet & dobest* or words to that effect (DJRU adding the 'Wit and Reason' phrase); but no manuscript rubric for **A** X, XI or XII mentions *dobet* or *dobest*.[8] Not only the promised guidance of Reason but also

---

[1] Hulbert, p. 223. [2] 'The Lost Leaf', p. viii.
[3] *Literary Relations*, p. 4. [4] pp. 221–2.
[5] 'Studies' II, pp. 23–24. I do not think that Dunning's explanation of the terms 'wit' and 'reason' as doublets (pp. 171–2) can be allowed. Other lexical considerations apart, their distinctness in *Piers Plowman* **A** is established by the poet's discrete allegorical use of them.
[6] The incipit occurs in eight **A** manuscripts, ChDH²JKRTU, of which DJRU are unmixed.
[7] Of the other unmixed **A** manuscripts V lacks rubrics and EHL break off before IX.
[8] For a discussion of **A** rubrics at those points see below, pp. 47–8.

the promised treatments of Do Better and Do Best are wanting. The confusion of views exposed at the beginning of this paragraph is not a necessary one; every indication, to an impartial view, is that **A** is unfinished. The evidence is, moreover, strong. Whilst the **A** incipits for X and XI might conceivably be scribal adoptions from **B** or **C** manuscripts (I do not think so), this cannot be the case with *secundum witte and Resoun* which (as far as I know) does not occur in any copy of **B** or **C**.[1] Even if the force of this evidence were not admitted the matter would be in doubt. And doubt is a poor foundation for a postulate.

If I have fairly represented the case against the single authorship of *Piers Plowman* and carried out my examination of it correctly it must appear that the quality notably absent from its arguments is logical necessity. Certain features of the texts of these poems were advanced as not attributable to a single poet. The applicability of some was shown not to have survived a growth in the knowledge of the subject; others originated in debatable or partial or illfounded critical judgements; some could be turned to the advantage of the argument only by recourse to logical fallacy. None of the inferences derived was of a compelling character in the light of what we know to be characteristic of the minds and careers of poets. All the features of the texts invoked against single authorship were at least as well explicable as originating in the work of a single poet. Since a miscellany of indifferent or positively bad arguments does not add up to a good argument I conclude that no genuine case against the single authorship of *Piers Plowman* has been made out from internal evidence.

There is, however, one last element in this use of internal evidence against the single authorship of *Piers Plowman* to be examined: the consideration of 'antecedent probability', strenuously advanced by Moore.[2] It is, essentially, the question whether in the literary circumstances of the fourteenth century a poem was more likely to be revised by its original author or by another man. To avoid the risk of misrepresenting him I quote Moore.

[1] The marginal entry containing this expression, at the end of VII in the **B** MS Cambridge University Library Ll. 4.14, was added by an annotator. The original rubric reads simply *Passus octauus*.

[2] 'Studies' I, pp. 179, 189; II, pp. 19–25. It is also invoked by Hulbert, pp. 215–16.

With regard to the antecedent probabilities of the case, I believe that no one who is moderately well acquainted with mediaeval literary history would contend that the continuation commonly called A[2] is a priori more likely to be the work of the author of A[1] than of some other writer, or that it is a priori less probable that a writer should have revised and expanded another man's work than that he should have revised and expanded a work of his own. All of these processes occur so commonly that one is intrinsically as probable as the other. ('Studies' I, p. 179.)

The first notable feature of this statement is the kind of pleading it exemplifies. To disagree would be to accept the imputation of being less than 'moderately well acquainted with mediaeval literary history'. The assertion is, of course, absurdly extreme, as becomes apparent when its implication is considered. If 'All of these processes occur so commonly that one is intrinsically as probable as the other', then any anonymous or insecurely ascribed Middle English poem is just as likely to have been written by several poets as by one, and further, since not every Middle English poem has yet found its Manly, any Middle English poem, though surviving only in a single form, may nevertheless be one of a succession of revisions by distinct authors. Moore was in my opinion the most cunning of the controversialists, but for this overstatement he loses points.

The second feature of the argument to note is that while it tacitly admits a certain quality of texture and style common to all the *Piers Plowman* poems it nevertheless denies the distinctiveness of their style, which 'was a style that not one man merely, but many men, had at their command';[1] there were 'many people who could write in this way'.[2] The authors of these opinions are not thinking of their four poets of *Piers Plowman* as the 'many men'. They have in mind the scribes whose additions to the text can be identified as spurious on genetic grounds. What they maintain is contrary to fact and does not bear examination. The striking feature of the genetic-ally identifiable scribal additions to *Piers Plowman* is their stylistic or alliterative inferiority.[3] Awkwardness, triteness, prolixity, over-explicitness, technical ineptitude, a general quality of tediously

---

[1] Moore, 'Studies' I, p. 187. [2] Hulbert, p. 216.

[3] For collections of such lines and passages see my A text, pp. 45–50, and G. H. Russell and V. Nathan, 'A *Piers Plowman* Manuscript in the Huntington Library', *Huntington Library Quarterly*, xxvi (1963), pp. 126–9.

inefficient iteration are their common character. They have the same qualities that mark the smaller scribal substitutions. There is thus, apart from anything else, a false basis to the assessment of antecedent probability.

But its worst feature is to misrepresent the event of which the probability is in question, by disregarding the special character of the present instance. So Hulbert, allowing that in our day a revision like that from **A** to **B** of *Piers Plowman* by a second author would be unlikely, asserted that

In medieval times conditions were the reverse of ours. In medieval England such revisions and expansions were a commonplace, and they were not usually by the original author.[1]

The expression 'such revisions' buries a consideration by which probability will be directly affected: the order of artistic magnitude of the poetry in question. For we are not concerned with the commonplace of chronicle or homily, or with the addition of pedestrian supplements to works of an incremental character, where no sweeping imaginative conception is involved. If this consideration is given weight Hulbert's instances[2] prove nothing about the probabilities in question in the case of *Piers Plowman*. The additions to Robert of Gloucester's *Chronicle*, *The Northern Homily Cycle*, or *The Prick of Conscience* by comparison are doggerel augmentations along implicitly prescribed lines; *The Seven Sages* with an elementary scheme and separable components invited substitution or improvement of its preexistent folktale material; the Towneley revisions of York plays have to do with an activity of communal character; the later version of Laȝamon is not a revision in our sense but a modernizing abridgement. We, however, are concerned with three poems each a great work of art, and with a situation where creative abilities of a major order were applied to a major theme. Here is then the true probability to be assessed: is it more likely that a revision and enlargement, found satisfying and successful and accepted as creating a new artistic whole by a body of opinion, some of it discerning and well informed, over several centuries, is the work of another man than the first author; or is it more likely that this retreatment is the work of that first author,

[1] p. 215. The exaggeration of the first sentence is to be noted.   [2] pp. 215–16.

revising his original composition according to a new and larger conception, sometimes for the better and sometimes (humanly) not so. I mean this to be a hard question, and I do not feel called upon to set down my own answer to it. My point is that in an opposition of these, the correct alternatives, there is no argument from antecedent probability against the single authorship of *Piers Plowman*.

In theory, notwithstanding the results of my examination of the case against the single authorship of *Piers Plowman*, the successful identification of multiple authorship of mediaeval poetry from internal evidence, even in the face of early ascription, is of course a possibility.[1] But I think one might fairly expect, in a clear case, that the evidence brought forward against single authorship would be such as to result in some measure of agreement among those who denied single authorship, and such agreement is signally wanting with *Piers Plowman*. I have made nothing of the difference of views on many details between those who would posit four or three or two authors, excluding John But. But this must raise doubts—which, of course, are explained by the character of the evidence and the arguments both. Moreover, and here is perhaps the strongest of all considerations: if a body of poetry were by more than one author, to account for it in terms of single authorship should in principle be possible only on the creation of critical hypotheses of an extreme character, based on assumptions of forbidding difficulty. Again this is not so with the *Piers Plowman* poems. The hypothesis by which these are explained as originating in a single poet is a good and convincing one, conforming in all respects to what we know of the processes of literature and the growth of a poet's mind.

[1] The use of internal evidence in the establishment of the Chaucer canon comes to mind. Cp. A. Brusendorff, *The Chaucer Tradition*, London, 1925, pp. 43ff, 433ff.

III

EXTERNAL EVIDENCE

If arguments from internal evidence have not yet excluded the possibility that one man wrote the three *Piers Plowman* poems, then the external evidence about their authorship has not been discredited and is worth re-examining. This evidence takes the form of a number of ascriptions either physically distinct from the poem or otherwise unmistakably distinguished from its text.

The fullest and one of the most ancient ascriptions occurs on the verso of the last integral leaf of a copy of the C version, Trinity College, Dublin MS D.4.1. As obviously the most important it must be examined first.

Memorandum quod Stacy de Rokayle pater willielmi de Langlond qui stacius fuit generosus & morabatur in Schiptoun vnder whicwode tenens domini le Spenser in comitatu Oxoniensi qui predictus willielmus fecit librum qui vocatur Perys ploughman.[1]

This statement the opponents of single authorship have variously attempted to devalue. Manly by implication dismissed it as 'in a fifteenth century hand (but not early)';[2] Moore somewhat more cautiously referred to it as 'written some time in the fifteenth century', but judged it to have less authority, and no earlier date, than a hypothetical note which he postulated as the necessary original of certain sixteenth-century ascriptions to a Robert Langland.[3] From outside the controversy the authority of the ascription has been denied on the grounds that its statements are anomalous: a legitimate son would necessarily bear his father's

---

[1] See plate I, facing p. 32. It has never been disputed that *fecit* here means 'wrote, composed', translating Middle English *made* (NED s.v. *Make* v.[1] 5a).

[2] *CHEL*, ii, p. 34. He was apparently following Skeat, who, on Dowden's information, and without inspecting the manuscript, had described Trinity College, Dublin MS D.4.1 as 'written in the fifteenth century, not very early' (*The Visions of William concerning Piers the Plowman*, iii, *Text C*, EETS 54, London, 1873, p. xlviii).

[3] 'Studies' II, p. 42. For discussion of these ascriptions to Robert Langland see below, pp. 37–46.

surname; because of opinions on illegitimacy expressed in *Piers Plowman* its author cannot have been a bastard; therefore, while the poet may have been a son of de Rokayle his name cannot have been Langland.[1] The ascription has even formed part of an argument that the author of the **B** version of *Piers Plowman* was John of Trevisa.[2] The pluralists' rejection of it included raising the reasonable question what is meant by the 'book called Piers Plowman'.[3] But the authority and the meaning of this ascription are distinct issues which must be separately examined; the necessary order of considering them will be obvious.

The ascription is physically authentic.[4] Manuscript and ascription are both very early; the hand of the ascription belongs to 'the beginning of the fifteenth century, perhaps even the turn of the fourteenth–fifteenth centuries'.[5] Even with due allowance for the latitude with which the date 'c. 1400' must be interpreted the time of writing of the ascription is within living memory of the composition of the poem. The writer of the ascription was thus chronologically able to have first-hand knowledge of the identity of the author of *Piers Plowman*. He was probably also advantageously located: the hand of the ascription is almost certainly that of a brief series of annals written above the ascription on the same last leaf,[6] which exhibit 'a considerable interest in the affairs of the South Wales Border, and a good deal of local knowledge'.[7] Where his

[1] O. Cargill, 'The Langland Myth', *PMLA*, l (1935), pp. 39–40. The fabric of Cargill's argument is weakened by its being based on a confusion of the dialects of the two Trinity College, Dublin *Piers Plowman* manuscripts (p. 38). This confusion was first pointed out by Brooks, pp. 152–3.

[2] Fowler, *Literary Relations*, pp. 202–3.

[3] So Moore, 'Studies' II, pp. 21ff; Hulbert, p. 216.

[4] The last leaf of the text of Trinity College, Dublin MS D.4.1, fol. 89, on the verso of which the ascription occurs, is the only surviving representative of its gathering and could thus, as far as the collation of the manuscript goes, be a supplement. But nothing in its appearance suggests that this is the case. The text on folios 88*b* and 89*a* appears to be in the same hand and ink (see plates II(*i*), (*ii*), between pp. 32–3). There seems no reason for considering folio 89 to be anything else but an integral part of the manuscript.

[5] According to the most expert modern opinion. It was so dated in 1951 (Brooks, p. 141) by Mr Neil Ker; he writes to me that he has not changed his view. Dr A. I. Doyle and Professor F. Wormald, whom I have also consulted, agree that the hand of the ascription is to be dated c. 1400. I am much obliged to all three for their generous and friendly help.

[6] Ker in his letter to me takes the identity of these hands for granted; Doyle writes 'I . . . have no doubt that the Langland note is in the same hand as the preceding memoranda'. The inks are identical.

[7] Brooks, p. 150. It may also be to the point that the dialect of the scribe of this copy, according to a recent study, is that of N.W. Gloucestershire near the Herefordshire border.

statements can be verified he appears well informed.[1] If, as may well be, he is responsible for certain marginal annotations to the text of the poem,[2] he also had some learning. His ascription thus scarcely merits Hulbert's contemptuous dismissal,[3] since he was evidently something more than a scribe. He was, in fact, both demonstrably knowledgeable and in a position to know of the matter in question.

The name of William de Langlond has not been verified. But the reasons advanced for believing that no man of that name existed are without force. Cargill's notion that in the fourteenth century a legitimate son would invariably take his father's surname is mistaken; there is no anomaly in the different surnames imputed to the father and son.[4] And there is certainly no justification for concluding that because one has not found a name more than once in fourteenth-century records there was no such person.[5] The evidence for accepting the existence of William de Langlond is the note which names him. This has substantive authority which is not diminished by the absence of verification.[6]

For this information I am indebted to Professor M. L. Samuels, whose kindness I take pleasure in acknowledging. See also his article, 'Some Applications of Middle English Dialectology', *English Studies*, xliv (1963), p. 94.

[1] See Moore, 'Studies' II, pp. 44ff; Cargill, pp. 47–48; Chambers, 'Robert or William', p. 461; Brooks, pp. 144ff.

[2] Doyle points out to me that the ascription hand is 'very like' the hand of marginalia on 'e.g. ff.13r–15v, giving fuller scriptural quotations and references'.

[3] 'In general, scribes' attributions of authorship haven't much weight' (p. 217). Hulbert's instances supporting this assertion are, as once before, not apposite. The attribution of religious texts to Rolle or of romances to Walter Map is the exact reverse of the present case, where famous poetry is ascribed to an unknown. In addition the assertion itself is debatable; cp. Brusendorff, p. 49, n. 3.

[4] This conclusion has emerged from the linguistic study of English surnames. The scholarship of the subject is summarized in the Introduction to P. H. Reaney, *A Dictionary of British Surnames*, London, 1958. See esp. p. ix: 'Throughout the Middle Ages surnames were constantly changing'; p. xliii: 'there is clear proof that [in the fourteenth century] many men still had no surname and that many were still not hereditary'. The mediaeval historians whom I have consulted agree that in the fourteenth century it was common for a man to be named after his native place, or a locality or holding, rather than after his father; further, indeed, that it was by no means unusual for a man to be known by several 'surnames'.

[5] This is Cargill's remarkable conclusion after an unsuccessful search for William Langland in the printed records of that century: 'If William Langland existed in the fourteenth century, he would have been easily located' (p. 42; see also p. 41). It is not clear whether Cargill's 'most thorough search' included the unpublished records of the century, which are extensive. But he should have known that those who figure in the documents of the time are generally persons of standing or at any rate property owners, or legatees, or litigants, or criminals. We do not know that the William Langland named in the ascription belonged to any of these groups.

[6] The *argumentum e silentio* must rest in a situation like the present one upon three distinct assumptions: that all records have survived; that surviving records are comprehensive; and

The next consideration is whether the ascription is deliberately false. For such a falsification I can by speculation find no motive that stands up to scrutiny except conceivably a conspiracy to conceal the true identity of the author of *Piers Plowman*;[1] even this I discount because I cannot believe that a note entered in the back of one manuscript in an obscure corner of the Southwest Midlands would achieve much to that effect. The ascription then seems necessarily

that the search in question was efficient. The danger of at least one of these assumptions can be illustrated from *Piers Plowman* studies. It will be recalled how Skeat was exercised because he had not found the name Langland in the West Midlands (*The Vision of William concerning Piers Plowman*, part iv, section ii, EETS 81, London, 1885, pp. xxiv–xxvii), and how Moore adduced that fact as evidence against single authorship: 'the name of Langland is unknown in Shropshire' ('Studies' II, p. 41). Moore's argument from the negative results of other men's searches has been dismissed (and the ground for Skeat's more judicious anxiety removed) by a recent discovery that the name Langland is actually well attested in Shropshire local records.

The credit for this discovery is due to the enthusiasm and energy of Mr J. Corbett of Much Wenlock, who very kindly communicated it to me and has handsomely authorized me to make it known.

The records are the muniments of the Childe family, preserved in the Birmingham Reference Library. Bundle 16 of these muniments contains at least five relevant documents which I note below. Information about nos. 2, 3, and 5 came to me from Mr Corbett; for knowledge of nos. 1 and 4, and otherwise for his most kind assistance, I have to thank the late Mr V. H. Woods, formerly Birmingham City Librarian. I am further obliged to my colleague Anthony Tompkinson for his expert help with this information.

(1) 28 September 23 Richard II (1399): Roger de Longelonde is a witness in a deed of gift by Hugh Dauys of Huggeley (Highley, co. Salop.) to Roger, son of John de Ardarne.

(2) 10 September 16 Henry VI (1437): John Longlonde grants Thomas Longlond his son a messuage and lands in Le Byrche in the manor of Huggele and a nook of land in Le Byrche in the manor of Kynelett (Kinlet, co. Salop.).

(3) 4 June 16 Henry VIII (1524): Thomas Longlonde grants Thomas Longelond his son a messuage and appurtenances in Le Birche in the manor of Higguley and a nook of land in Le Birche in the manor of Kynlet and six acres of land in Le Birche. (The deed also names a William Longlond son of Thomas and a William Longlond brother of the grantor.)

(4) 8 December 20 Elizabeth I (1577); Richard Longland of Cuddyngton (Cuddington, co. Bucks.) grants to Thomas Longland son of William Longland his own messuage called le Hunte Howse and a nook and six acres of land now or lately in the tenure of the said William Longland, lying in Higgeley and Ernwood (Earnwood, co. Salop.), including land in Le Byrche.

(5) 2 April 23 Elizabeth I (1581): Thomas Longlande 'thonger' (?the younger) of the parish of Kinlet, husbandman, mortgages to Humfrey Dallowe and William Mason of Kinlet a tenement called the Hunte House and various named pieces of meadow and pasture including the meadow called the Longland and arable lands in Le Birche in the parish of Kinlet and in Hidgley.

It is still too early to say what the full implications of this evidently important discovery will be. But for my assessment its force is quite clear. By its sharp reminder that the present state of knowledge is by no means necessarily final it constitutes an impressive warning against drawing unfavourable inferences about the quality of existing evidence from the absence of other evidence.

[1] Cargill seems to have this possibility in mind (pp. 41–42).

either true, or a mistake made in good faith. That leaves the question whether its author, although otherwise he was knowledgeable, in this particular recorded erroneous information, perhaps 'a baseless rumor',[1] or else perhaps a mistaken inference from the notorious line in the **B** version (XV 148) which, read backwards, can produce *wille longe londe*.[2] There are considerations which make both these possibilities seem more remote than they might appear at first sight.

For instance, if it is supposed that the name William Langland came into existence because the writer of the Trinity College, Dublin ascription took **B** XV 148 to embody an unknown author's full cryptogrammatic signature,[3] then it necessarily follows that he went on to assign a flesh and blood father to this presumed identity. It is hard to accept the imputation of such a procedure to a person who in other particulars, such as the circumstances of the flesh and blood father, has shown himself correctly informed. Or supposing that the writer of the ascription knew that a son of Stacy de Rokayle had written *Piers Plowman*, but was ignorant of that son's name, how likely would he be to fix on this line of the poem as obscurely revealing the hitherto unknown name of the son of a man whom he knew? Or supposing the writer of the ascription to have been wholly ignorant of the identity of the author of *Piers Plowman*, and to have searched the poem for a clue (even, with more than common perseverance, reading each line backwards), in what circumstances would he be likely, when coming upon **B** XV 148 and finding there concealed the name of a William Langland whom he knew, and whose father's name and condition he also knew, to ascribe the poem to him?

The first implication of these considerations is that to be credited with a (verifiable) flesh and blood parent a person named William Langland must actually have existed. Since Cargill's several objections to his existence are unfounded it seems necessary to accept this. The second implication is that the writer of the ascription knew William Langland to be the son of de Rokayle— in effect that, being knowledgeable in other matters he was

---

[1] Hulbert, p. 217. Note how 'baseless' begs the question. Presumably Hulbert meant 'hearsay'. But even hearsay, while not evidence in a court of law, can be true.

[2] So Cargill, p. 41.

[3] This would not be inconceivable, but the likelihood seems minute. See pp. 65ff. below, esp. p. 69, n. 2.

knowledgeable also in this one. The third, certainly the most exciting, is also the most serious: that the writer of the ascription, knowing the circumstances of de Rokayle and the name of his son, would scarcely have ascribed the 'book which is called Piers Plowman' to the latter unless he knew this man to have been at least capable of writing it. For it seems a primary likelihood that in the fourteenth century as at other times a man was not credited with the authorship of a large body of poetry of wide and lively contemporary interest without some grounds, certainly not merely because a quantity of accurate information about his father was available. The sum of these implications is then that a William Langland, the son of Stacy de Rokayle, not merely existed but was known by the writer of the Trinity College, Dublin ascription to have been concerned with writing poetry.

One feature of the ascription particularly rewards scrutiny: that is its form as a statement. Our modern interest has centred on the information which it affords about the authorship of *Piers Plowman*; in the ascription the clause conveying this appears by its position of lesser importance, a secondary element. The most prominent components of the ascription are matters of regional and personal rather than literary concern: parentage, status, locality. The ascription reads as if, indeed, the man who wrote it was primarily interested not in the identity of the author of *Piers Plowman* but in his credentials, those, as it were, of someone whose name and activities he already knew. For such a reading it is not hard to find speculative support. The author of *Piers Plowman* was evidently not a metropolitan notable like Chaucer; as far as his name getting into the national records was concerned he may well have been a nonentity. But that his activities were totally unknown in his time seems essentially improbable. It is not in the nature of things that a man should be engaged over several decades in the composition of a major work of great immediate moment and early wide currency[1] without his preoccupation being known to at least some persons. Meanwhile for many conceivable reasons such a man might well be reticent about his origins, and, moreover, by his reticence arouse curiosity about them. On these considerations the true force of the ascription might be: here is recorded information about the

[1] For this the evidence is the existence of a manuscript tradition of the **A** version.

parentage and background of the William Langland who is known to have written *Piers Plowman*.

In any case the ascription of the 'book which is called Piers Plowman' in Trinity College, Dublin MS D.4.1 is a genuine, near-contemporary document, composed within a single lifetime of the event which it records. Its author, as regards both time and place, was in a position to know that which, by setting it down, he claimed to know. In those particulars which are verifiable it is accurate. It contains no anomalous or intrinsically improbable statements. No immediate reason appears for presuming its ignorance or error in the unverifiable part, and no good reason suggests itself for thinking it a deliberate falsification. It seems, then, evidence to be taken seriously, indeed of a kind to which historians would accord respect. Unless, therefore, it is shown to be false its correctness is to be presumed.

One particular in the Trinity College, Dublin ascription, the baptismal name of the author, is supported by two other pieces of ancient external evidence. The earlier of these is the well known ascription by John But which constitutes the end of **A** XII in one of the three manuscripts where that passus appears.[1] Unless this coda is a hoax by the poet (which is hard to conceive) it is external evidence, to be dated from its content before the deposition of Richard II. The relevant part of But's conclusion is the statement that 'Will composed what is copied here, and other works as well about Piers Plowman and many people in addition'.[2] How authoritative is this ascription? Chronologically But was in an excellent position to know what he was writing about. Just how knowledgeable he actually was it is less easy to determine.[3] His statement is externally corroborated in only the one particular of the poet's baptismal name. Agreement on this particular between But

---

[1] Discussed by H. Bradley, 'Who Was John But?', *MLR*, viii (1913), pp. 88–89; E. Rickert, 'John But, Messenger and Maker', *MP*, xi (1913–14), pp. 107ff.; Moore, 'Studies' II, pp. 30–33; Cargill, pp. 52–54.

[2] Wille . . . wrouȝthe þat here is wryten and oþer werkes boþe
Of peres þe plowman and mechel puple also. (**A** XII 99–102)

[3] Rickert, holding that she had identified But as a King's Messenger, argued (pp. 113–16) that a man in such an office would be very likely to know who wrote *Piers Plowman*. While her identification may be correct it is not, unfortunately, to be accepted without hesitation. Not all the other possibilities mentioned by her (p. 107, n. 2) can be so easily excluded as she seems to believe. Indeed Cargill's discovery of connexions between de Rokayles and Buts (pp. 52ff.) might seem more important than the Rickert identification.

Memorandum quod Stacy de Rokayle pater Willi de Langlond qui
Stacius fuit generosus & morabatur in Schipton under Whitwode
Tenens Dni le Spenser in comitatu Oxon qui p̃dictus
Willielmus fecit librum qui _____ vocatur PERYS Ploughman

1. Trinity College, Dublin MS D.4.1 fol. 89*b*

And cam and toke man kynde / and by cam fol needy
he was so needy oars ye bok / in mony sondry places
yat he seyde in his sorowe / on ye selue rode
Bothe fox and foul may / flee to hole and creope
and ye fiche hath fynnes / to flete wiþ ye reste
yeer neode hath y nome me so / yat y mot neode a byde
and soffre sorowes soure / yat schal to loye turne
for thy beo not a baptiste / to bidde and beo needy
Syth he yat wrousht al ye worlde / was wylfulyche needy
Neuere non so needy / ne non so poure deyde
When neode hadde vndernome me thus / anon y fel a slepe
and mette fulle meruey lousliche / yat in mannes forme
Antecrist cam yenne / and al ye crop of treuthe
Torned hit tyd vpseden / and ouer tilte ye rote
and made fals to spryngge and sprede / & spede mennes needes
In eche contrey yer he cam / he cutte a wey treuthe
and gert Gyle growe yer / as he a god were
ffreres folowede yat feend / for he yaf hem copes
and religion reuerede hym / and rongen here belles
al ye couent yo cam / to welcome yat tyraunt
and al his as weel as hym / saue onliche foles
ye wyche foles weren gladdere to deye
yan lyue lengur sithe leaute / was so rebuked
and a fals feend Antecrist / ouer al folc regnede
That were mylde men and holy / & no meschief dredden
Defyeden al falsenesse / and folk yat hit vsede
and what kynge conforted hem / knowyng here gyle
yei corsede and here consail / were hit clerk or lewede
Antecrist this sone hadde / hondredes at his banere
and pryde bar yat banere / boldeliche a boute
With a lord yat lyueþ / aftur lykynge of his body
And cam a zeins conscience / yat kepere was and gyour
Ouer kynde cristene / and cardinale vertues
y conseile conscience yo / comes why me ze foles
In to vnite holychurche / and hald we vs there
and cry we to kynde / yat he come and defende
Ous foles fro ye feondes lymes / for peres loue ye plouhman
and cry we on al ye comune / yat yei come to vnite
Ther to a byde and bykere / a zeyns belials children
kynde herde yo conscience / and come oute of ye planetes
and sent forthe his foreyours / feueres and fluxes

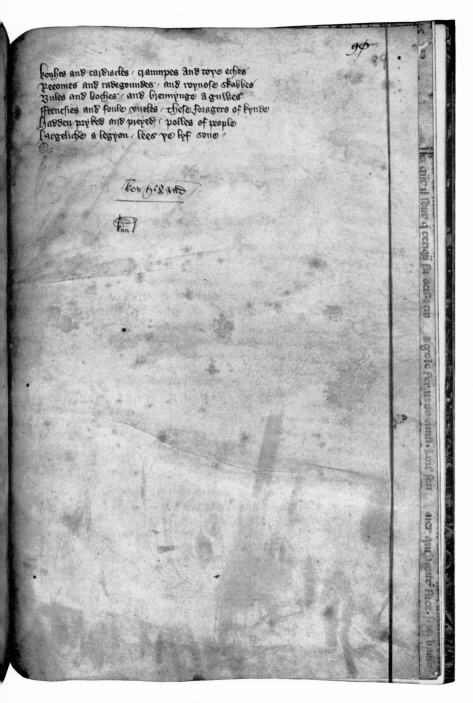

ffoulles and caudiacles · crampes and toys etches
 Recomes and radegoundes · and roynose skabbes
Bules and boches · and bremynge a guttes
ffrencies and foule conetes · these foragers of kynde
Hadden prysed and preyed · polles of people
Largeliche a legyon · lees po leef cono

Ton Herard

Ton

II. (ii) Trinity College, Dublin MS D.4.1 fol. 89a

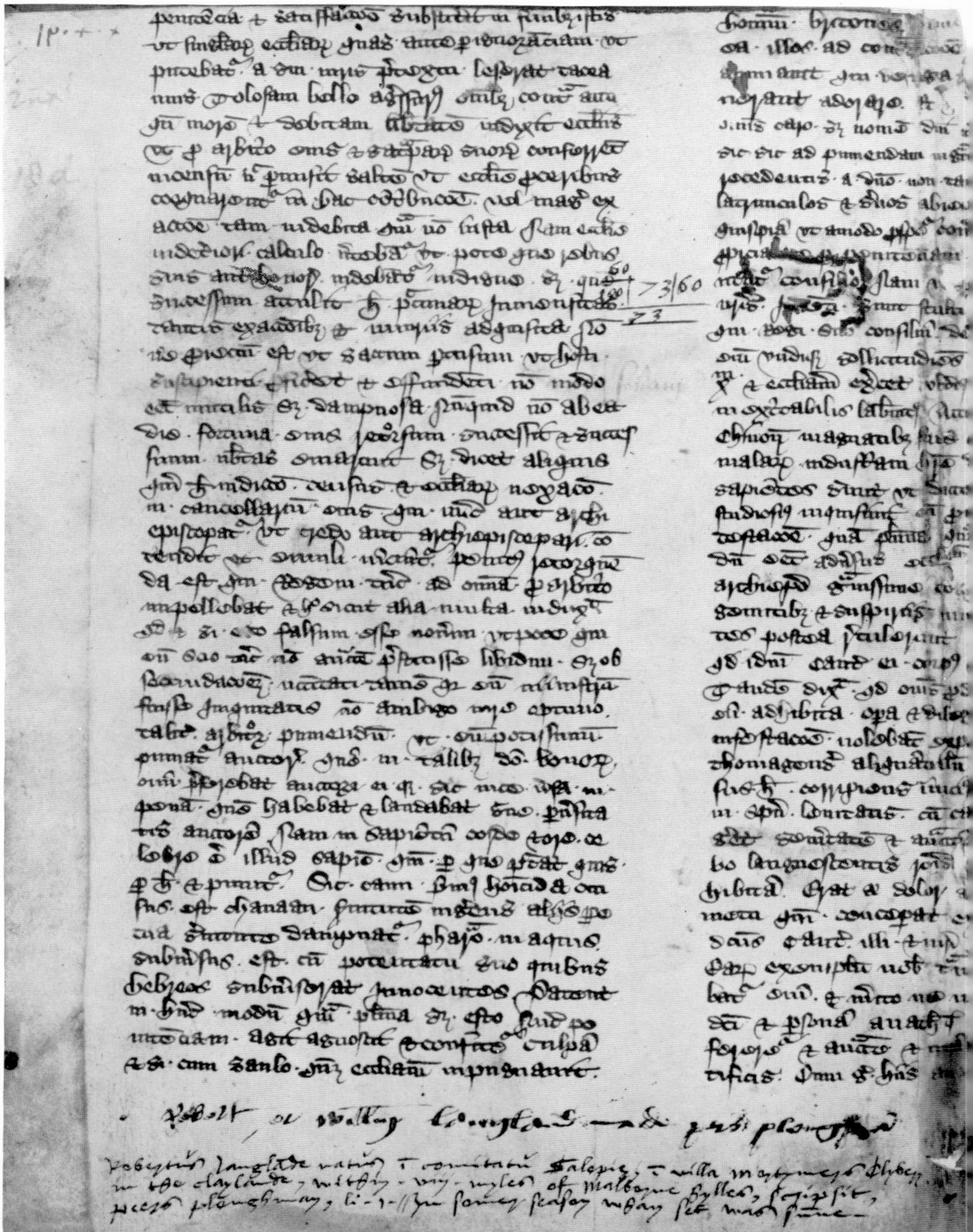

III. Huntington Library MS Hm 128, front endpaper

and the writer of the Trinity College, Dublin ascription does not, of course, itself necessarily signify that But was writing from external knowledge. For But might, in ignorance of the author's name, have inferred identity between him and Will the Dreamer, and might have extended his ascription to 'other works as well about Piers Plowman' because he was aware that Will the Dreamer figured in these also. There is, however, one circumstantial detail in But's obituary which cannot have originated in inference from the texts of the *Piers Plowman* poems, his report that the poet's death was sudden and unexpected: *ere wille myȝte aspie Dep delt him a dent* (**A** XII 103, 104). This report is either purely fanciful, or implies knowledge. The first alternative cannot, of course, be excluded, but does not commend itself. The author of a notable contemporary poem would (it appears to me) scarcely have been described as dead unless the fact of his death was known. And if that fact was known there would seem little point to embroidering detail about it; there is, moreover, in all ages a kind of piety which should have restrained even a meddling poetaster from such invention. On these grounds, and having regard to the time when John But wrote, the greater evidential likelihood seems to be that he wrote of the poet's death from knowledge, truthfully. And if he knew that the author of *Piers Plowman* was dead and how he died, there is a strong probability that he also had knowledge of his identity.

Meanwhile it must be clear that the authority of John But's ascription cannot be held to be quite primary. The possibility of his information about the author's name being the product of inference cannot be excluded; and one cannot, I suppose, be sure that the circumstance of the author's sudden death was not invented. Thus the agreement of But's ascription with another ascription of primary and substantive authority could be fortuitous. Nevertheless, this agreement is an undeniable fact. And But's ascription, again containing no impossible or anomalous statement, is by a man who could, chronologically, have known the author, and is thus the oldest external evidence about the authorship of *Piers Plowman* available to us. Moreover the assessment of the value of his evidence must exclude irrelevant associations. The stigma of spuriousness attached to **A** XII as poetry must not be allowed to extend to But as a witness about authorship. For all his wretched verse he was capable of knowing and telling the truth; we cannot show that he did not do so; and what he tells us agrees with information from a very different kind of source.

The third of the ancient ascriptions supporting that in the Trinity College, Dublin memorandum occurs in a manuscript combining texts of **A** and **C**, Liverpool University Library MS F.4.8 (Ch) dated c. 1425, which reads at the end *Explicit liber Willielmi de petro le plowȝman*. This is the only final explicit in any manuscript which designates an author, and the only rubric at any point in any version to name an author unmistakably.[1] When the manuscript where it occurs is compared with the two others of similar composition, T and H[2], with which it shares an exclusive common ancestor,[2] its explicit appears as a calculated departure from both the reading of its family tradition and the usual form.

The authority of this ascription is again not finally determinable, for here too the name William which it contains could be derived from inference that the names of Dreamer and poet were identical. It could, however, equally well come from near-contemporary knowledge.[3] Deciding between these alternatives is evidently impossible. Meanwhile the formulation of this rubric was almost certainly a deliberate and serious act. The manuscript is in a good tradition, implying a succession of careful scribes. This raises the question how likely one of these would be to record mere personal inference in such a prominent and categorical form? In any event, however, the name in the rubric agrees with the baptismal name of the author in the Trinity College, Dublin ascription, and with that given by John But.

The situation so far is that an ascription with historical authority of the first order is corroborated in one particular by two other ascriptions comparably ancient but each to some extent lacking

---

[1] For rubrics of another type, which may possibly contain an ascription, see below, p. 35.

[2] Trinity College, Cambridge MS R.3.14 (T) ends simply *Explicit*; B.M. Harleian MS 6041 (H[2]) has no explicit. The genetic relation is almost certainly [(TH[2])Ch].

[3] The manuscript is dated c. 1425. But the independent tradition of Ch may well be much older. The exclusive common ancestor of its subgroup [(TH[2])Ch] was necessarily in existence somewhat before c. 1400 when T was copied, to allow time for the intervening stage of transmission during which the exclusive common ancestor of the genetic pair (TH[2]) was copied. The rubric with the ascription does not appear to have been in this manuscript; but it could have entered the particular tradition of Ch at any stage of Ch's descent from the exclusive common ancestor of [(TH[2])Ch].

primary authority because part or all of the information it contains could have been deduced from the text of the poem. Thus evidently the supposition that the 'book called Piers Plowman' is by William Langland rests mainly on the evidence of the Trinity College, Dublin note. Meanwhile the agreement of all these ascriptions with respect to the poet's baptismal name, even having regard to the possibility that it might in one or both instances be fortuitous, will evidently have a very different effect on the conclusions reached from that which would be exercised by any serious, that is, un-accountable, disagreement.

The next question is whether such unaccountable disagreement exists; that is, whether the remaining external evidence about the authorship of *Piers Plowman*, which conflicts with that in the Trinity College, Dublin note, is genuine and authoritative and thus discredits this note.

What might appear to be the earliest conflicting evidence about authorship occurs in the rubrics of five C manuscripts which read at the end of Passus X *Explicit visio Willielmi .W. de Petro le ploubman*.[1] The point of conflict is the letter *.W.* which, if it signifies a surname, stands for a different one from the *de Langlond* of the Trinity College, Dublin ascription.

By the presence of the *.W.* these explicits differ from the usual rubric at this place in C and corresponding places in A and B, of which the type is *Explicit visio Willielmi de petro* etc. Because of its ambiguity the typical rubric is not necessarily evidence of authorship. For it could mean either 'the vision which William composed' or 'the vision which William dreamed', whereas because of the presence of the *.W.* the rubric of XYIUD seems un-ambiguous, since, if *.W.* stands for a surname,[2] *Willielmus .W.* was identified as someone more specific than the Dreamer whose surname, unless it was Longelonde, is not revealed. If, then, *.W.* stands for a surname, this apparently more specific rubric is an

---

[1] They are: Huntington Library MS Hm 143 (X); Bodley MS Digby 102 (Y); University of London Library MS S.L.V.88 (I, formerly 'Ilchester'); B.M. Additional MS 35157 (U); and Bodley MS Douce 104 (D).

[2] Whether it does so seems questionable on general grounds. Initials were used in the fourteenth and fifteenth centuries to denote surnames, but usually (I am informed) in documents such as domestic accounts where their value would be readily apparent. There would seem to be little point in ascribing a poem to an otherwise unknown 'William W.'

ascription. Its authority and character must therefore be examined.

Although this rubric is five times attested its distinctive form is, for a start, almost certainly the result of a single act of writing. The five copies where it occurs are at the point in question the representative members of the *i* subgroup of C manuscripts [(XYIP²) UD].[1] The reading *Willielmi .W.* was thus inferably the reading of the exclusive common ancestor of this subgroup, and is therefore attested, in effect, by a single manuscript. This fact does not, of course, invalidate it as evidence; it makes clear the degree of support.

Whatever else the significance of this rubric may be it can at once be ruled out that the *.W.* which distinguishes it was 'written as a mere random guess'.[2] Scribes had their shortcomings, to be sure, but it is barely conceivable that one would bestow a letter intended to imply an unspecified surname on a poet simply by caprice. It can also be excluded that the *.W.* originated in inference from the poem, since there is nothing in the text of any version to give rise to it. The designation *Willielmi .W.* is thus either an ascription made from external information (correct or otherwise) or a scribal error.

Supposing the rubric to be an ascription where the *.W.* stands for a surname, the person responsible for the initial was chronologically in a position to have known the identity of the author.[3] Thus it would be possible that the surname beginning with *W* which he intended to signify was actually the author's, and that ascriptions to Langland are incorrect. There would be a further possibility, that the difference of identities suggested by the discrepancy was not real, since in the fourteenth century when a man's second name was derived from a locality of origin or association (as de Langlond evidently was) it was not infrequent for him to be known by several 'surnames'. Thus it would not be impossible that a William de Langlond was otherwise called William Wychwood.[4]

---

[1] When fully represented the subgroup comprises nine manuscripts, probably thus: ⟨[(XYIP²)OLB]UD⟩. But OLB have earlier transferred to a **B** exemplar, and the discrepancy suggested by the absence of the rubric from P² is only apparent. For in P² there was, at this point, an interruption of copying, with, possibly, a change of hands; and although a space was left for rubrication between Passus X and XI the rubric was never supplied.

[2] As Moore suggested ('Studies' II, p. 35).

[3] Again because, in view of the date of at least one of its descendants, the exclusive common ancestor of the manuscripts where the rubric occurs must have been in existence before c. 1400.

[4] See Skeat, *C Text*, p. xxxvii.

Simply from the point of view of the disagreement between *de Langlond* and *.W.*, the authority of this rubric is indeterminable. It might be correct and the Trinity College, Dublin note in error; or the reverse; or the poet might have gone by two surnames.

But the possibility that the rubric in XYIUD is an ascription is put most grievously in doubt by the ease with which its distinctive *.W.* is explicable as scribal error. It will be recalled that this *.W.* probably came into existence by one act of copying in the exclusive common ancestor of a subgroup of C manuscripts. Thus a single operation of error could have brought it into being. A very commonplace process, which would account for its existence and which the local text suggests, is attraction to a letter previously copied. Even the source of subconscious preoccupation with this letter can be identified as concern about how, in a rubric, to distinguish *w*, which did not have a true capital form.[1] The agent of the error could have been either the scribe who inserted the rubricator's guide, or the rubricator himself. In either event the *.W.* would before long have the authority of handsome lettering, red ink, and its enclosing dots to ensure its being recopied. Even these latter would be explicable as the result of the next scribe mistaking a cancellation of the original error by subpunctuation for punctuation intended to set off the letter.

Thus the value of the rubric of XYIUD as evidence of authorship is insignificant. That it can so easily be explained as something else diminishes the likelihood of its being an ascription. If it were an ascription its disagreement with the Trinity College, Dublin ascription would not necessarily relate to a difference of identities. In any event its authority does not compare with that of the partly verifiable and circumstantial statement in the Trinity College, Dublin manuscript. It does not seriously challenge this, and indeed because of its dubious character can be of no use in the establishment of the identity of the author of *Piers Plowman*.

The only serious challenge to the ascription in the Trinity College, Dublin manuscript is offered by a cluster of ascriptions dating from the first half of the sixteenth century and associated with John Bale,

---

[1] Another of Moore's suggestions ('Studies' II, p. 35) that 'an erasure immediately before the word *de* in the colophon may have been interpreted by a copyist as a blurred *W*', will hardly commend itself to textual critics.

which disagree with the older evidence about the baptismal name of the author of *Piers Plowman*. There are six of these.[1] They differ somewhat in wording, but all agree that the author of *Piers Plowman* was called Robert Langland. The entry in Hm 128 will serve as the type:

Robertus Langlande natus in comitatu Salopie, in villa Mortymers Clybery in the claylande, within .viij. myles of Malborne hylles, scripsit, peers ploughman, li.j. // In somer season whan set was sunne—

These ascriptions naturally played a major rôle in the controversy.[2] Since their only necessary conflict with the Trinity College, Dublin ascription is in the baptismal name of the author, here is the point where their authority must be tested.

This conflict was dismissed by Skeat as having arisen through someone's wrong inference about the author's name from a corruption of the opening line of **B** VIII 1, *Thus yrobed in russet I romed aboute*, where in one manuscript known to Skeat *yrobed*(v. l. *robed*) was misread as *y Robert* (*B Text*, p. xxviii). His suggestion was accepted by Manly[3] but not, once the controversial pitch had mounted, by Moore. To account for the sixteenth-century ascriptions Moore hypothesized that they were derived from a note of the same general character as the Trinity College, Dublin ascription, but probably of equal or greater antiquity, which, though now lost, had been seen by Nicholas Brigham, one of the informants whom Bale acknowledges in his *Index*.[4] Moore's hypothetical note (and thus Brigham's information) were for him 'more trustworthy' than the Trinity College, Dublin ascription. This, he argued, was because—supposing the original name to have been either Robert or William—it was more probable that original Robert would have

---

[1] One occurs on the front endpaper of a **B** manuscript, Huntington Library MS Hm 128 (see plate III, facing p. 33); four in John Bale's manuscript published by R. L. Poole, *Index Britanniae Scriptorum . . . John Bale's Index of British and Other Writers* (Oxford 1902, pp. 383, 509, 510); and one in Robert Crowley's preface to his impressions of the **B** version, printed in 1550 (*S.T.C.* (1926) p. 456, nos. 19906–19907ᵃ); the relevant parts of this preface were published in Skeat, *B Text*, pp. xxxiiff.; Moore, 'Studies' II, p. 35; Chambers, 'Robert or William', p. 430. Two others naming a *Robert* Langland, in Bodley MS Laud Misc. 581 (discussed by Chambers, op. cit., p. 432), and in the Library of the Society of Antiquaries MS no. 687 (see below, p. 43, n. 3) are probably later and derivative.

[2] The main discussions are by Moore, 'Studies' II, pp. 35ff.; Cargill, pp. 42ff.; Chambers, 'Robert or William', pp. 430ff.

[3] *CHEL*, ii, p. 34.

[4] 'Studies' II, pp. 35–40.

been ousted by William, in view of the force of **B** XV 148, *my name is longe wille*, than that original William would be displaced by Robert because of a scribal error *robed*] *robert*, for the rejection of William in favour of Robert required ignorance or disregard of **B** VIII 124 *Here is wille wolde ywyte*.[1]

Unless all three particulars in the sixteenth-century ascriptions are the products of inference (the surname from **B** XV 148, the birthplace from **A** XII 105,[2] and the baptismal name from a form of **B** VIII 1 or **A** IX 1), which seems a remote possibility, the implication is that these ascriptions derive at least in part from an earlier source.[3] Because they contain information about the poet's birthplace and lack information about his paternity it is unlikely that this source was the Trinity College, Dublin ascription. The conflict is, then, between two distinct documents, one surviving as far as we know first hand, the other more recent by about a century and a half, and necessarily derivative.

In such an opposition the actually more ancient testimony would seem, *prima facie*, to have the greater authority not only because its writer, living when he did, was in a better position to know, but also because the later statement, being derivative, might like any text embody modifications, unconscious or deliberate, acquired in at least a century and a half of transmission. Thus the two ascrip-tions cannot really be compared on equal terms. For while it is possible that the sixteenth-century ascriptions reproduce exactly the information of an earlier, even a very early note, it is also possible that this is not so: that they consist partly of information from an earlier source, and partly of something else. They contain one scribal error, probably originally unconscious and presumably copied in ignorance.[4] The crucial question is whether they differ

---

[1] 'Studies' II, pp. 42–44. Moore was, I am inclined to think, generally more interested in confusing issues than in assessing the respective authority of these names. His hypothesis and accompanying arguments deserve to be read for their own sake, as a remarkable specimen of sophistry. His mission in the controversy was evidently to sow doubt on all sides, creating a favourable state of mind for the reception of arguments from internal evidence.

[2] So Cargill (pp. 43–44) argued.

[3] This inferentially necessary source takes on a new character from the discovery of the Langland names in Shropshire records. Kinlet is the adjacent parish to Cleobury Mortimer.

[4] The distance of *viij* miles between Cleobury Mortimer and the Malvern Hills is in-correct through loss of *x* or corruption of *xx* to *v* at the beginning. So Moore, 'Studies' II, pp. 40–41.

from their putative source in a second, more important respect, that is in testifying for the baptismal name Robert.

To this question it is for a start relevant that the sixteenth-century ascriptions undoubtedly originated in an active search for the identity of the author of *Piers Plowman*.[1] This fact implies readiness to exercise judgement and assess evidence, a state of mind not necessarily favourable to the simple reception and transmission of received information. Indeed, unmistakable evidence that a situation where judgement and decision were called for arose in the search is afforded by another, older ascription also in Hm 128, written above that already quoted from the manuscript, which reads *Robert, or William langland made pers ploughman*.

It is, secondly, relevant that the search was, if not concerted, at least carried out with consultation. This is clear not only from the general similarity of the six fuller ascriptions but also, in particular, from the part played in the search by an indeterminate but probably fairly small number of manuscripts possibly in close genetic relation, one of which has survived as Hm 128.

The first evidence of the limited nature of the search is a variant for Prologue I, *soft*] *set*, found in the text of Hm 128, in the second ascription on the endpaper of that manuscript, in Crowley's text, in Crowley's preface where the opening lines of the poem are quoted, and in one of the ascriptions in Bale's *Index*,[2] but not else-where.[3] Next there is the error of distance, *viij* for *xviij* or *xxiij*, found in the second ascription of Hm 128 and three Bale ascrip-tions.[4] Then there is the spelling *Malborne* common to the ascription in Hm 128 and two of Bale's.[5] Finally there is the date 1369 which

---

[1] As Crowley's preface by itself would suggest. Natural curiosity about the author of an evidently considerable poem would indeed have been supplemented by the awakening antiquarian interest, and the religious conditions of the times. *Piers Plowman* manuscripts were much handled, read and annotated in the sixteenth century. At least one manuscript copy of each version was made in the first half of that century (Bodley MS Digby 145, Cambridge University Library MS Gg.4.31, and B.M. MS Royal 18.B. XVII). Catholics and Protestants alike found contemporary application in the text.

[2] That *Ex domo Guilhelmi Sparke*, Poole, p. 509.

[3] Unless the variant *soft*] *sote*, glossed *warme*, in another Bale ascription (*Ex collectis Nicolai Brigan*, Poole, p. 383) reflects it, as could well be. In that case, so also does the Latin one immediately following, on the same page, where *caleret* presumably translates *warme*.

[4] Brigham's two, and Sparke's.

[5] Those credited to Brigham. This appears to represent a genuine form of the name. See A. Mawer and F. M. Stenton, *The Place-Names of Worcestershire*, Cambridge, 1927, p. 210.

is represented in the unique text of Hm 128 for XIII 270 as *a thowsand and thre hundryd syxty and nyne*, and in one of Bale's ascriptions.[1]

It will have been observed that while no single one of these particulars is found in all the Bale ascriptions and Crowley's text and Hm 128, nevertheless in some one of the distinctive features Hm 128 agrees with each of the ascriptions or with Crowley's text. This inclusion of Hm 128 in each agreement implies that Hm 128 belonged to someone at the centre of the search,[2] and therefore also that the search was not as wide as Bale's four entries might seem to suggest. This second implication is supported by the extent of agreement over the reading *set*. Such agreement between Hm 128 and Crowley's text is not surprising in view of an otherwise indicated possibility of genetic relation between Hm 128 and the lost manuscript from which Crowley printed.[3] But that the text of Hm 128 and Crowley's text and two of the four ascriptions which cite a first line agree in reading *set* implies that not many more than three manuscripts were consulted, for otherwise, in view of the rarity of this variant, greater disagreement would certainly have shown. The whole nexus of agreement establishes the character of the search: that it was not very extensive, or very thorough, or necessarily wholly enlightened.

The evidence of the endpaper of Hm 128 is that it proceeded in

---

[1] That *Ex Ioanne Wysdome medico*, Poole, p. 510. This line of Hm 128 differs by erasure and correction of its last three words in another hand from the archetypal reading of **B**, *A thousand and pre hundred twies twenty and ten* (two manuscripts, Bodley Laud Misc. 581 and Rawlinson Poet.38 which read *tweis thretty* must on genetic grounds embody corrections here; another, B. M. Additional MS 35287, reading *thries twenty*, shows the actual correction), and indeed from the reading of all **B** manuscripts known to me. The date 1369 also appears in Hm 128 in Arabic numerals beside the line.

[2] Whether to the owner of the hand which wrote *Robert, or William langland made pers ploughman*, whom I have failed to identify; or to John Bale if, as Skeat (*A Text*, p. xxxv) and Chambers ('Robert or William', p. 434) believed, the fuller ascription on the endpaper is in his hand; or to John Wysdome, with whose information the text of the manuscript agrees about the date 1369.

[3] The variational group HmCr is attested by some 30 agreements in unoriginal readings, and forms part of the larger variational group WHmCr attested by some 60 agreements of the same sort. The genetic situation is obscured by the very frequent 'correction' of Hm during or soon after the process of copying. Thus the first twelve lines of the poem, where the reading *set* occurs, are over erasure in a hand found elsewhere in the text as the main hand. It is therefore indeterminable whether the agreement of HmCr in reading *set* resulted from vertical or lateral transmission. But that Hm acquired this reading very early is not in doubt.

two phases. The first, in which the surname Langland, the rival baptismal names[1] and possibly the birthplace were collected, is signified by the shorter Hm 128 ascription recording the alternatives. On the indication of a corresponding offset on the opposed flyleaf this entry was made after the manuscript was rebound in about 1540.[2] The second phase, during which the decision for Robert was reached, presumably ended when the fuller and positive ascription in Hm 128 was made, or 1550 when Crowley's first impression was issued, or the date when Bale made the first of the entries in his *Index*, whichever was the earliest.[3]

In any case the limited circumstances of the search and the evident connexion of the other five ascriptions with Huntington MS Hm 128 contain one further, important implication: that in the choice between Robert and William as the correct baptismal name of the Langland whom Crowley, Bale, and their informants believed to have written *Piers Plowman* only a single act of decision was involved. The ascriptions to Robert Langland, comprising the four in Bale's manuscript *Index*, the one in Crowley's preface and the one on the endpaper of Huntington MS Hm 128, are no more than separate records of this; they are thus in effect texts descending from one exclusive common ancestor. Whether this was edited, or partly formed, by the deliberate substitution or adoption of Robert for William is now the question.

If such an event occurred this must, on present evidence, have been as Skeat originally suggested (*B Text*, p. xxviii) because the searchers were misled by a manuscript in which the opening line of the first passus of the Vision of Do Well read for *yrobed* or *robed* some corruption like *I Robert* or *Robert*. Skeat was led to this explanation by knowledge of such a corruption in one manuscript, a copy of **B**, Corpus Christi College, Oxford MS 201, which, otherwise heavily sophisticating the opening of the passus, reads

---

[1] Even Moore did not suggest that the note implied a choice between two actual identities ('Studies' II, p. 42).

[2] Evidence of rebinding and the date are given by R. B. Haselden and H. C. Schulz of the Huntington Library: see *Huntington Library Bulletin*, No. 8 (1935), pp. 26–27. The hand of the entry has been dated 'mid-sixteenth century' by Robin Flower and C. J. Sisson. See Chambers, 'Robert or William', p. 434, n. 1.

[3] The *Piers Plowman* entries in the *Index* are not precisely datable, but they do not appear to be among the earliest in the manuscript. See Poole, pp. xixff.

& *y Robert in rosset gan rome abowhte*.[1] Subsequently a copy of **A**, now Library of the Society of Antiquaries MS no. 687, came to light, which at the corresponding point reads *þus Roberd in Russet I Romyd abowtyn*.[2] The discovery of a second instance of this corruption more than doubled the force of Skeat's explanation, for the evidently independent occurrence of *Robert* in two unconnected manuscripts proves what could be only presumed from a single instance, that it is a typical coincident variation, of a kind which, having occurred twice may easily have occurred more often, and therefore may have been present in manuscripts that have not survived. What has not yet been made known is that this independent coincident corruption in these two surviving manuscripts is accompanied by independent sophistication at the later point in the same passus where the Dreamer Will is named (**B** VIII 124; **A** IX 118), with the coincident intended effect of suppressing his name. Instead of *Here is Wille wolde ywyte* Corpus Christi College, Oxford MS 201 reads *Fayn wolde y wete witt*; Antiquaries' MS 687 reads *To heryn fawen woldy wetyn*. Whether or not this sophistication occurred at a stage of transmission subsequent to the corruption of *yrobed* it clearly establishes that the scribal variant 'Robert' of VIII 1 was twice independently taken to be a name conflicting with Will, and one of superior authority.[3]

From these indications it was thus evidently possible not merely for the variation *yrobed*] *I robert* to occur coincidentally, but also for more than one fifteenthcentury scribe to accept the variant seriously as a name. It is then not hard to accept that a manuscript with such a variant could have passed through the hands of the antiquaries concerned with the Robert ascription; this manuscript, moreover, might not have contained the name Will at **B** VIII 124;[4] and it could evidently have given rise to a mistaken conclusion or

---

[1] *Robert* is written *Robt* with a stroke through the *t*. But the transcription is not in doubt; it can be confirmed from the scribe's practice at V 469 as Chambers ('Robert or William', p. 436) pointed out.

[2] This is the manuscript described by Chambers (p. 436) as belonging to Mr Allan H. Bright.

[3] Nor is it generally known that the Antiquaries' MS also contains, in a late sixteenth- or seventeenth-century hand, the entry *The author Robert Langland a cheife disciple of John Wickliffs*.

[4] For Moore ('Studies' II, pp. 42–44) the presence of the two names in one passus was an argument against the possibility of the name *Robert* coming from VIII 1.

confirmed a mistaken notion that the poet's baptismal name was Robert. Whether Bale and his associates actually saw either of the surviving manuscripts where the corruption occurs cannot be determined.[1] But that other manuscripts containing the corruption once existed is an unquestionable possibility, almost a probability of textual criticism. It is even possible to speculate that a lost manuscript, a genetic connexion of Hm 128 and Crowley's original, reading like these two *set* for *soft*, possessed the corruption. For in VIII 1 Crowley's first impression has a misreading, *throbed* for *yrobed*, and at the same point Hm 128 reads *robed* in another hand and ink over erasure of a longer word. The suggestion is, of course, that this word was corrupt in an exclusive common ancestor, and that another of its descendants, now lost, also reading *set*, read *y Robert* for *yrobed*.

It remains to ask why the sixteenthcentury antiquaries, with a choice of the names Robert and William before them, should have decided for Robert. Crowley at least could scarcely have avoided knowing that the name Will occurred three times in his poem; it is hard to believe that he left his associates in ignorance of this information. It cannot, therefore, safely be maintained that their eye was caught by Robert in a prominent position at the beginning of a main division of the poem, and that in consequence they unreflectingly assumed Robert to be the name of the author.[2] More probably, possessing information about the surname and birthplace, as well as a copy of the poem which contained both baptismal names, they would have concluded that one of these must belong to the author and the other to a fictive creation of the author's. It is possible to imagine how their deliberation went. Here was a poem in which the name Will occurred three times, and Robert only once. Moreover on one occasion (**B** XV 148) the Dreamer unambiguously said *my name is longe wille*. But on two other occasions (**B** V 62 and VIII 124) he was referred to in the third person; and on all three he was engaged with imaginary characters (reduced to tears of contrition by Reason's sermon, engaged with Thought; conversing with a tongueless, toothless *sotyl thinge* of many names). This is not, the reasoning might have

---

[1] Both bear marks of sixteenth-century handling. But neither reads *set* in Prologue 1.
[2] So Chambers, 'Robert or William', pp. 436–7.

gone, how an author reports of his actual self. Whereas, in a passage between visions (**B** VII 139–VIII 67) distinguished from preceding matter by a marked change of tone and concerned throughout with actualities, at VIII 1 this new narrator Robert, referring to himself in the first person, recounted how he disputed with a pair of friars, a very real and dangerous class of actual men. Thus Robert might have seemed to possess reality, and William, therefore, to be his creation. And such a conclusion, attained by reasoning sound enough within its limits of available knowledge,[1] would appear firm ground for correcting an ascription, from ancient, popish and therefore barbarous times, to William.

I have no doubt that in any context except the *Piers Plowman* controversy the information set out above would be accepted as establishing the strongest presumption that the name Robert in the sixteenth-century ascriptions originated in inference from a corrupt form of the first line of the Vision of Do Well, and because it appeared to have superior veracity first challenged and then displaced an earlier received name William. I have compared the sixteenth-century ascriptions to copies of a single text which might embody corruptions of that original; for a textual critic the demonstration of the possibility of a particular error by reference to two explicable instances of its occurrence would be an overpowering argument that the same reading in a third, otherwise questionable instance, if similarly explicable, was also corrupt by the same process. But the problem is one of assessing external evidence and must be finally expressed as such.

We have then a disagreement in one particular between an ascription of c. 1400 and one of c. 1540–1550. Of these the older, which in itself would be accepted as historical evidence of the first order has, on external considerations, superior authority, is partly verifiable, and receives some contemporary and near-contemporary support. The discrepant particular in the more recent (whatever ancient original we presume it to have had) is, meanwhile, susceptible of explanation by reference to an actual, twice-instanced course of error, and this, moreover, of a kind by its nature likely to have occurred more often. Because of this possibility, in terms of

---

[1] They could hardly have known about the convention of signature often observed in mediaeval dream-vision poems. On this see IV, pp. 53ff. below.

which the discrepant particular may be the product of mistaken inference (such as elsewhere demonstrably occurred) from misleading information (instances of which have survived) the authority of the more recent ascription does not begin to match that of the older one.

The results of the assessment so far may now be summed up. Of all the external evidence known to exist the most authoritative is the Trinity College, Dublin ascription which states that a William Langland of named paternity *fecit librum qui vocatur Perys ploughman*. There is contemporary support for his baptismal name in the coda added to the **A** version by John But, and in the explicit of one **C** manuscript. A rubric in five manuscripts containing the expression *Willielmi .W.*, where the *.W.* might stand for a different surname, is easily explicable as originating in a single scribal error. The sixteenth-century ascriptions to Robert Langland of Cleobury Mortimer, while supporting the surname of the Trinity College, Dublin ascription and adding a not impossible detail about the poet's birthplace,[1] are with regard to the baptismal name of highly questionable authority because their Robert may be a ghost raised by a scribal error.

The best evidence we have then testifies to William Langland as the author of the 'book which is called Piers Plowman'. But, as has earlier been indicated, in the history of the subject the name of the poet is almost a side issue compared with the question whether one man or several wrote the three versions. What is the 'book called Piers Plowman'? For however correct and true the evidence of the Trinity College, Dublin ascription may be, it might refer only to the **C** version in a copy of which it appears. Did the writer of the ascription have in mind that one, or some two, or all forms of the poem? The answer to this question must lie in the terms of the time when the ascription was written. Such terms survive in the rubrics of the *Piers Plowman* manuscripts.

When these are examined it is evident that the designation 'Piers Plowman' was applied not to the *Visio* but to the whole poem. This is clear from final explicits. There one **A** manuscript

---

[1] This has not been verified (Moore, 'Studies' II, p. 40, n. 4) but the presence of Langlands in the neighbouring parish of Kinlet will oblige us, henceforth, to treat it seriously.

calls the poem *liber petri plouman*;[1] another *tractus de perys plowman*.[2] Eight **B** manuscripts call it *dialogus petri plowman*;[3] a ninth **B** manuscript, *visio Petri ploughman*.[4] In **C** manuscript explicits the designation appears five times, as *liber vocatus Pers ploghman*;[5] *liber de Petro ploughman*;[6] *liber . . . de petro le plowȝman*;[7] *tractatus . . . piers plowman nominatus*;[8] and *Peeres plouheman*.[9] These indications are the more impressive for the complete absence of contrary evidence. No rubric in any manuscript of any version suggests that a poem has ended with **A** VIII or its equivalent in **B** or **C**. The absence of such suggestion from **B** and **C** is perhaps to be expected. What is certainly notable is the indication of the rubrics in **A** manuscripts that *Visio* and *Vita* were viewed as a single poem,[10] and that in the fourteenth and fifteenth centuries the **A** version was regarded as incomplete, an implication already present in the existence of manuscripts combining the **A** and **C** versions.[11]

[1] Bodley MS Douce 323 (D). Manly ('Authorship', p. 13) apparently did not know of this copy.

[2] B.M. Harleian MS 3954 (H³) (Combined **B** and **A** texts). Manly's rejection of the evidence of this manuscript ('The Authorship', p. 13) is not to be allowed. Despite its **B** beginning it would have been identified in the fifteenth century as a 'short' form of the poem.

[3] Bodley MS Laud Misc. 581; Cambridge University Library MSS Dd.1.17; Gg.4.31; Ll.4.14; B.M. Additional MS 35287; Trinity College, Cambridge MS B.15.17; Oriel College, Oxford MS 79; Newnham College, Cambridge Yates Thompson MS (LCGC²MWOY).

[4] Huntington Library MS Hm 128 (Hm).

[5] B.M. Additional MS 35157 (U).   [6] Bodley MS Douce 104 (D).

[7] Liverpool University Library MS F.4.8 (Ch) (Combined **A** and **C** texts).

[8] The Duke of Westminster's MS (W) (Combined **A** and **C** texts).

[9] Huntington Library MS Hm 137 (P).

[10] Moore ('Studies' II, p. 21) misrepresented the situation when he wrote that 'The colophon which in all of the MSS stands at the junction between the *Vision* and the *Vita* shows that the A-text was regarded as consisting of two poems.' The rubrics there mark the end of one vision and the beginning of the next. In the single instance where a rubric might seem to imply the contrary, the **A** manuscript Douce 323, which reads at the beginning of X *Primus passus in secundo libro*, the special meaning of the term *secundo libro* is indicated by the final rubric, *Explicit liber petri plouman*, which must apply to the whole *Piers Plowman* text in the manuscript since Piers does not figure *in secundo libro*. Such a use of *liber* for a part of the whole book occurs also at the beginning of the **B** manuscript Cambridge University Library Gg.4.31: *Hic incipit Petrus P*[cropped] / *de visione liber primus*. Another **A** manuscript, Rawlinson Poet.137, with a contemporary first rubric *Hic incipit liber qui uocatur pers plowman*, has the common *Explicit hic visio willielmi* etc. at the end of VIII, distinguishing the *visio* as a part of the whole *liber*. The combined **BA** manuscript Harley 3954, ending with **A** XI, which has the title *Perys Plowman* in the main hand, shows clearly in all its rubrics that this title applies to the whole poem.

[11] Of the seventeen **A** manuscripts six (ChH²KNTW) received supplementation from **C**. One (H³) combines the **B** and **A** versions. One **A** manuscript (V) is not rubricated. Three (EHL) break off in the *Visio*. There remain ADJMRU. Of these six four (AJRU) show in

For those who commissioned the copying of **A** manuscripts or directed their rubrication or copied them for their own use the 'book which is called Piers Plowman' did not then in the four-teenth and fifteenth centuries mean the *Visio*, in **A** or in any version. Indeed, quite the contrary, these men evidently understood a dis-tinction between the part and the whole, between a book and its sections. The indication of all rubrics in all manuscripts is that the vision of Piers was regarded as one of a series of visions which belonged together in a single book.

It is, secondly, evident from the rubrics of *Piers Plowman* manu-scripts that the designations 'vision' or 'dialogue' or 'treatise' or 'book which is called Piers Plowman' and even plain 'Piers Plowman',[1] were applied impartially to all versions of the poem, and that the writer of the Trinity College, Dublin ascription did not necessarily or even probably have in mind the particular version in a copy of which he recorded his information, indeed would not have understood our differentiation between **B** and **C**. Of course those who concerned themselves with the poem in the fourteenth and fifteenth centuries did not distinguish the versions as we understand these. They had not conceived modern notions of editing or com-pared copies to establish the existence of three artistically sub-stantive forms of the poem. But they were not, therefore, necessarily fools. That they had a notion of 'better' readings is clear from the occurrence of correction and cross-copying. It is also clear, as has been shown, that they distinguished between a short and a fuller form of the poem, that is to say between **A** and the other versions, because the incompleteness of the former was evident to them. They did not distinguish, apparently, between **B** and **C**, because

their rubrics before **A** IX and XI or XII evidence of the rubricators' sense of incompleteness. Having announced at the beginning of Passus IX *Hic incipit vita de dowel dobet & dobest*, four (AJRU) call Passus X *Primus passus de dowel*; two (AR) call XI *Passus secundus de dowel*; the three (JRU) which contain Passus XII call it *Passus tercius de dowele*. Meanwhile no **A** manuscript incipit for X, XI or XII mentions *dobet or dobest*. As to final rubrics, two of these six manuscripts (JU) are incomplete at the end. One (D) has a conclusive explicit (see p. 47, nn. 1 and 10 above). One (A) reads at the end noncommittally *Amen Amen*. But two show unmistakably a sense that the poem is not finished. M (the Antiquaries' MS 687), which heads Passus IX *prologus de dowel dobet & dobest*, lacks incipits for X and XI and has at the end of XI *Explicit prologus de dowel dobet & dobest*. R (Rawlinson Poet.137), the manuscript which contains John But's conclusion, and heads the poem *Hic incipit liber qui uocatur pers plowman*, has a final rubric *Explicit dowel*.

[1] The **B** manuscript Cambridge University Library Dd.1.17 (C) has a running title *Piers Plowman* in the main hand.

either or both these forms satisfied them, conferring a sense of imaginative unity centred in the dominant symbol after which they named the poem, and a sense of the unity of substance on which Owst so properly insisted;[1] and evidently these unities defined for them the 'book which is called Piers Plowman'. It seems no better than wayward to refuse the contemporary evidence that the various forms of the poem, in so far as they were identified, were regarded as variant manifestations of a single poetic entity.

There is thus in the practically uniform indications of all the ancient evidence that has come down to us a tradition in the accepted sense of the term:[2] one of the unitary character of the *Piers Plowman* poems. If this tradition does not often raise the question of authorship the best reason for the omission may be that it takes single authorship for granted. For we cannot assume that fourteenth- and fifteenth-century readers were not interested in the question; evidence to the contrary has survived. One *Piers Plowman* rubric, occurring in an early fifteenth-century manuscript which combines the **A** and **C** versions,[3] reads at the point of juncture *Passus nonus de visione & vltimus et hic desinit Et de cetero tangit auctor de inquisicionibus de Dowel Dobettre & Dobest.* Another manuscript at least as old, also combining **A** and **C** versions, reads unambiguously at the end *Explicit liber Willielmi de petro le plow3man.*[4] The attention of the composers of both these rubrics embraced the author; both assumed single authorship of what they perceived to be distinct parts of a single whole.[5]

The evidence of rubrics with respect to the meaning of 'Piers Plowman' in the Trinity College, Dublin ascription is borne out by that of John But. The authority of his ascription can be

---

[1] *Preaching in Medieval England*, Cambridge, 1926, pp. 295–6.

[2] Moore ('Studies' I, p. 180) and Hulbert (p. 216) use 'tradition' with a lexically unauthorized private meaning. See *NED* s.v. sb. 4 and 5. If the term is properly employed, then any 'tradition' of single authorship must have changed character in 1550 with the appearance of Crowley's edition, after which date the matter became one of information available in print. What Moore and Hulbert were actually discussing was whether, since the first printing of the poem, this has generally been held to be the work of one author. Cp. Bloomfield, 'The Present State', p. 220.

[3] National Library of Wales MS 733 B.

[4] Liverpool University Library MS F.4.8. Discussed above, p. 34.

[5] The author of the rubric in the first manuscript was very likely the person responsible for its combination of versions, which was carried out with elaborate conflation. In the case of the second awareness of the distinction is registered in adjustments of passus numbers. See my A text, pp. 2, 40–41.

questioned as I have indicated,[1] but its meaning is not really open to doubt. In his statement *Wille . . . wrouȝthe þat here is wryten* the object clause can refer only to the A version. For wherever the John But coda begins, in the genetic group $\{<[(TH^2)Ch]D>RU\}$ it was almost certainly added either to the exclusive common ancestor of the genetic pair RU or to a manuscript between that ancestor and R.[2] In the tradition of this group there is no evidence that the two parts of A were ever copied separately, and good reason to think that they were not, but that, as all surviving A manuscripts indicate, the A version was transmitted from the beginning as a physical unity.[3] Thus except in *ex parte* argument *þat here is wryten,* 'what is copied here', means either A Prologue–XI (if But wrote all of Passus XII), or A Prologue–XI with some indeterminate part of XII. As for the 'other works about Piers Plowman and many other people', these could conceivably be lost poetry which that description would fit; but since the description fits also the B and C versions the dispassionate interpretation, and the best because it dispenses with conjecture, is that the 'other works' are the additional matter in the B or C version or in both. Between B and C versions decision is impossible, since the plural *werkes* need refer simply to the plurality of visions in the longer forms of the poem. But it must be emphasized that the C version is not to be excluded on consideration of date.[4] John But's ascription thus refers to A and B, or A and C, or, since B and C were not distinguished in the fourteenth century, probably to all three ver-sions. However viewed it has evidential value, recording either genuine knowledge or a fourteenth-century belief that the *Piers Plowman* poems were by a single author.[5]

---

[1] Above, p. 33.

[2] Which was the case is not determinable, since U is imperfect at the end. But chrono-logically the former alternative seems somewhat more probable.

[3] See my A text, pp. 27, 42–44.

[4] As Rickert (pp. 115–16) argued in the belief that C had been composed in or after 1393, therefore after the death of her John But (*ob.* 1387), and therefore by another man than the author of A. Leaving aside consideration of the necessity of her identification, it is now generally agreed that Skeat's assignment of a late date to C was mistaken, and that it was probably composed c. 1385. For a recent discussion see M. W. Bloomfield, *Piers Plowman as a Fourteenth-century Apocalypse*, New Brunswick (N.J.), 1962, p. 90.

[5] Even if purely speculative it would be evidence (which may be important) that a fourteenth-century reader of *Piers Plowman* identified Dreamer and poet. On this point see IV, pp. 53ff. below.

The existence of John But's coda implies, incidentally, that he regarded the short form of the poem as lacking an ending. It is not without relevance that his coda, with its ascription, occurs in the only **A** manuscript which begins *Hic incipit liber qui uocatur pers plowman*, promises a *vita de dowel dobet ⁊ dobest* after the *Visio*, and ends *Explicit dowel*. Whatever the authority of John But's information, from this circumstance it appears that he acquiesced in the name given to the **A** version, sensed the incompleteness of the copy he was handling, and saw fit to record, in his pious memorial to its poet, that this man had written more on the same subject.

Three independent ancient sources give the baptismal name of the poet as William. The one of the three which further specifies the surname as de Langlond has primary historical authority. The authority of the apparently conflicting suggestion of *William .W.* and of the ascription to Robert Langland are shown to be suspect. The *Piers Plowman* of the ascriptions which survive the assessment is, in modern terms, severally the **A** version and at least one other (John But), the **A** and **C** versions (the Liverpool University Library MS explicit), and inferably the **B** or **C** version (since although the Trinity College, Dublin ascription occurs in a manuscript of the latter version the man who wrote it is unlikely to have distinguished between **B** and **C**). But on the showing of rubrics the designations 'book' or 'dialogue' or 'treatise of Piers Plowman' were applied impartially to all versions. Further, while the difference between **A** and other versions was perceived, the several versions were evidently regarded as variant manifestations of one work comprising a number of clearly defined parts; the satisfying and desirable form was that which held them all: the 'book called Piers Plowman'. There is no evidence of an ancient view of multiple authorship, but some that single authorship was taken for granted. As far as the name of the author goes, there appears to be no good reason for thinking that this was anything else but William Langland.

IV

SIGNATURES

If this assessment is to be complete it must include one further consideration: the implications of the fact that the first-person narrator in each of the three versions of *Piers Plowman* is called Will. This consideration has not been admitted to preceding discussions[1] because the occurrences of the name are by my classification neither external evidence of authorship, since the name is an element of the text, nor internal evidence, since its existence is absolute, not contingent on identification by the critical faculty.[2] The names are, however, a fact both historical and literary, and in both respects relevant to the question of authorship.

Inevitably their significance was disputed in the controversy. The essential issue was whether the recurrent naming of the Dreamer was to be identified as a single author's signature. This was expressed in various assertions and denials. A fourteenth-century poet writing a dream-vision poem would or would not name his dreamer after himself; Will the Dreamer who reports and figures in the three versions was or was not a total fiction; he was or was not to some greater or lesser degree an autobiographical projection of a single author; if in the *Visio* of the earliest version he was such a projection, he was subsequently kept in being by a succession of continuators. How easily this issue in its various forms could be confused, if only by biographical irrelevancies, will be apparent to anyone who reads the literature of the subject. A decade of discussion passed before the matter under debate received clear formulation: whether the intention of the allusions to Will was 'to claim all the texts as the work of one man' of that name, and (if such a claim was establishable) whether it was genuine or a

---

[1] Indeed the presence of the name in the text has actually been allowed to diminish the credit of some external evidence: see above, pp. 33, 34.

[2] This circumstance is, of course, the result of my classification, and has no bearing on the import of the names with respect to authorship.

deliberate misuse of 'the name and reputation of the first "Will"'.[1]

In the atmosphere of the controversy the evidential value of these names was thus doubly open to challenge. Today, if my assessment of the case against the single authorship of the *Piers Plowman* poems is correct, this is no longer so. If no authoritative evidence, internal or external, exists for believing in a succession of *Piers Plowman* continuators, and if the correct showing of the external evidence is that William Langland wrote the three versions, the possibility of fraudulent claims does not arise. The first question, however, survives: whether the poems contain the deliberate signatures of this William Langland. Its answer is in the first instance a matter of literary history: was it an established practice, a convention, for fourteenth-century authors of dream-vision poems to sign their work by naming the dreamer-narrator after themselves? Is there an *a priori* likelihood that the name Will is an author's signature? It is in the second instance a matter of literary criticism: do the disposition and function of the name in the three versions and the activities imputed to its bearer appear designed to encourage at least nominal identification of dreamer and poet?

It is straightway beyond question that some French and English authors of dream visions, like Dante and Jean de Meun before them, signed their poems.[2] The practice of signature, meanwhile, was not confined to this genre, and the extent to which it was followed suggests that poets of any standing were not so dedicated to anonymity as is, apparently, sometimes believed.[3] The popular thirteenth-century *trouvère* Rutebeuf signed fifteen of the fifty-five poems known to be from his hand;[4] in the fourteenth century

[1] R. W. Chambers, 'The Three Texts of "Piers Plowman", and their Grammatical Forms', *MLR*, xiv (1919), p. 131. For earlier discussions see J. J. Jusserand, '*Piers Plowman*: the Work of One or of Five', *MP*, vi (1909), p. 279; Chambers, 'The Authorship of "Piers Plowman"', *MLR*, v (1910), pp. 29–31; Moore, 'Studies' II, pp. 25–31; and more recently Hulbert, pp. 216–17.

[2] To assert this fact and indicate its bearing on the question of authorship is no novelty. See J. J. Jusserand, *L'Epopée Mystique de William Langland*, Paris, 1893, p. 63; Chambers, 'The Three Texts', p. 131; Preface to A. H. Bright, *New Light on 'Piers Plowman'*, Oxford, 1928, pp. 17, 19ff.; and for the fullest demonstration, 'Robert or William', pp. 439ff. This last article, completed before the war and published posthumously in 1948, seems to me to be Chambers's greatest contribution to the discussion. Fowler appears not to know of it.

[3] Cp. E. Hoepffner, 'Anagramme und Rätselgedichte bei Guillaume de Machaut', *ZfRP*, xxx (1906), p. 401.

[4] E. Faral and J. Bastin, *Oeuvres Complètes de Rutebeuf*, Paris, 1959, i, p. 34.

Guillaume de Machaut claimed authorship, by one or another means, of ten of the eleven *dits* confidently attributed to him.[1] Eustace Deschamps named himself between fifty and a hundred times in the corpus of his poetry. Froissart, similarly, was not backward in claiming his verse.[2]

Signatures in the work of these poets take a variety of forms. There is of course the open name;[3] in addition a variety of crypto-grams were evidently fashionable. There was the anagram, if not introduced at any rate put in vogue by Nicole de Margival,[4] and extensively used by Froissart.[5] Machaut employed not only ana-grams,[6] but also a code of alphabetical numbers.[7] To open signature and the anagram Deschamps added acrostics[8] and syllabic disarrangement with a punning effect.[9] Guillaume de Deguileville inserted a macaronic poem acrostically revealing his name in the second version of his *Pèlerinage de la Vie Humaine*.[10] In *Vox Clamantis* Gower identified himself by a syllabic cryptogram.[11]

A concomitant of the signing of poetry in this period was the involvement of the author in the action of his poem. The Lover in the *Roman de la Rose* was little more than a personified abstraction;

---

[1] Hoepffner, 'Anagramme und Rätselgedichte', p. 402. Where the signature is absent a reason for this is sometimes confidently inferable: Hoepffner, loc. cit.; Faral and Bastin, pp. 34–35.

[2] A typical example might be the beginning of *Le Débat dou Cheval et dou Levrier*, *Oeuvres de Froissart: Poésies*, ed. A. Scheler, Brussels, 1870–2, ii, p. 216; see also n. 5 below.

[3] So, for example, Rutebeuf (p. 53, n. 4, above); de Machaut, *Le Jugement dou Roy de Navarre*, *Oeuvres de Guillaume de Machaut*, ed. E. Hoepffner, *SATF*, Paris, 1908ff., i, ll. 573, 1499, 4199–200; and others (p. 56 below).

[4] *Le Dit de la Panthère d'Amours*, ed. H. A. Todd, *SATF*, Paris, 1883, ll. 2630ff. On de Margival's influence see E. Hoepffner, 'Les Poésies Lyriques du *Dit de la Panthère* de Nicole de Margival', *Romania*, xlvi (1920), pp. 204–30, esp. pp. 226ff. See also Brusendorff, p. 48, n. 3.

[5] See N. R. Cartier, 'Anagrams in Froissart's Poetry', *Mediaeval Studies*, xxv (1963), pp. 100–8.

[6] See Hoepffner, 'Anagramme und Rätselgedichte', passim, also Machaut, *Oeuvres*, i: *Le Jugement dou Roy de Behaingne*, ll. 2055ff.; ii: *Remède de Fortune*, ll. 4257ff.; *Le Dit dou Lyon*, ll. 2172ff.; iii: *Le Confort d'Ami*, ll. 3965ff.; *La Fonteinne Amoureuse*, ll. 31ff.

[7] *Oeuvres*, ii: *Le Dit de L'Alerion*, ll. 4801ff.

[8] *Oeuvres Complètes de Eustache Deschamps*, iv, ed. de Queux de Saint-Hilaire, *SATF*, Paris, 1884, p. 222; v, 1887, p. 164.

[9] *Oeuvres*, iii, 1882, p. 381; iv, p. 114.

[10] Chambers, 'Robert or William', p. 446. The poem is most readily inspected in Lydgate's translation. See *The Pilgrimage of the Life of Man*, ii, ed. F. J. Furnivall, EETS ES 83, London, 1901, pp. 621–3.

[11] *The Complete Works of John Gower*, ed. G. C. Macaulay, iv, Oxford, 1902, prologue to bk. i, ll. 19ff.

fourteenth-century imitations of that model often have a more particularized narrator who is, furthermore, made in the image of the poet. This is particularly notable in the case of Machaut who may have established the practice;[1] there is not one of his poems where he does not assign himself a rôle, the size of which increases as his career proceeds;[2] various of his attributes as a participant in the narrative or dramatic situations of his creation can be related to his actual biography.[3] The first-person narrator of Machaut's *dits*, represented as awake, moves easily back and forth across the boundaries of possible reality; he converses impartially with personified abstractions or with representations of actual historical personages; he is addressed or referred to by name during the action,[4] or, continuing the first person's voice without interruption, he offers a puzzle of letters or numbers which contains the poet's name.[5] The represented waking experience of such a mixture of reality and fantasy by a personage named after the poet is found most often in the work of Machaut simply because this comprises a substantial number of long allegorical narratives. It also occurs, however, in Huon de Meri's *Tournoiement de l'Antechrist*,[6] and notably in Gower's *Confessio Amantis*.[7] In these poems the narrator, who reports that he has undergone, while awake, experiences necessarily and evidently fictitious, makes a point of identifying himself as the writer. It was thus evidently a practice for a poet, presenting a fantastic action of his own creation through the voice of a first-person narrator, to establish his authorship by giving that narrator his own name, which he might reveal cryptically like Machaut or openly as Gower does.[8]

That the practice of signature by this means amounted to a convention is further evidenced by its occurrence in a variety of poems, light or grave, where the action is represented as experienced in a dream, but which otherwise do not differ essentially from, for instance, Machaut's *dits*. In such poems the dreamer-narrator, even

---

[1] Hoepffner, *Oeuvres*, i, pp. lvii–lix.   [2] *Oeuvres*, i, pp. iiff.; ii, pp. lx–lxi.
[3] *Oeuvres*, i, pp. ii, xviff.   [4] p. 54, n. 3, above (*Roy de Navarre*).
[5] p. 54 above.
[6] *Li Tornoiemenz Antecrit*, ed. G. Wimmer, *Ausgaben und Abhandlungen aus dem Gebiete der Romanischen Philologie*, lxxvi, Marburg, 1888. Chambers cites this example.
[7] This was another of Chambers's instances.
[8] *The English Works of John Gower*, ed. G. C. Macaulay, ii, EETS ES 82, London, 1901, *Confessio Amantis*, bk. viii, ll. 2320–1, 2908.

when nameless, is likely to be represented as the writer.[1] Often, however, he is given the poet's identity. This may be conferred on him indirectly, by implication, when, though not openly named, he is represented as possessing attributes identifiably those of the poet.[2] The dreamer may reveal his identity by offering a cryptogram of his name, which turns out to be that of the poet.[3] The dreamer may openly give the poet's name as his own.[4] He may give it on request during his vision.[5] Personages in his vision may address him by the poet's name.[6] Such personages may refer to him in their conversation by the poet's name.[7] In all these instances the

[1] E.g. in *Le Songe Vert*, ed. L. Constans, *Romania*, xxxiii (1904), p. 538, ll. 1776ff.; *Le Songe du Castel*, ed. R. D. Cornelius, *PMLA*, xlvi (1931), ll. 20–21; Froissart, *Le Paradys d'Amours*, *Oeuvres*, i, ll. 1713ff.; *Le Joli Buisson de Jonece*, *Oeuvres*, ii, ll. 2ff.; *Le Temple d'Onnour*, op. cit., ll. 25ff.; *Le Livre du Tresor Amoureux*, *Oeuvres*, iii, ll. 615ff., esp. ll. 734ff.; Honoré Bonet, *L'Apparicion Maistre Jehan de Meun*, ed. I. Arnold, Paris, 1926, ll. 1527ff.; Chaucer, *Book of the Duchess*, ll. 1331ff.; *Parliament of Foules*, l. 118 (*The Works of Geoffrey Chaucer*, ed. F. N. Robinson, 2nd edn., Cambridge, Mass., 1957).

[2] Thus the dreamer in the first version of de Deguileville's *Pèlerinage de la Vie Humaine* has a 'godfather' Saint William (*Le Pelerinage de Vie Humaine*, ed. J. J. Stürzinger, London, 1893, ll. 4153–5); similarly in the second version (Lydgate's translation, *The Pilgrimage of the Life of Man*, i, ed. F. J. Furnivall and K. B. Locock, EETS ES 77, 83, 92, London, 1899–1904, l. 1308); there also his father is named (ll. 9438ff.); in de Deguileville's *Pèlerinage de l'Ame* the dreamer again has a 'godfather'; there is also a letter about his person containing an acrostic of his name (*Le Pelerinage de l'Ame*, ed. Stürzinger, London, 1895, ll. 1039ff.; 1593ff.) (these are Chambers's examples). In Watriquet de Couvin's *Li Dis des IIII Sieges* the dreamer's patron is identifiable (*Dits de Watriquet de Couvin*, ed. A. Scheler, Brussels, 1868, ll. 431ff.); so also in Froissart's *Joli Buisson de Jonece* (*Oeuvres*, ii, ll. 230ff.). In Bonet's *Apparicion Maistre Jehan de Meun* the dreamer identifies his actual house, and his station in life (prose ll. 89ff.). The dreamer in Grandson's *Songe Saint Valentin* reveals the name of his mistress by acrostic (*Oton de Grandson: Sa Vie et ses Poésies*, ed. A. Piaget, Lausanne, 1941, ll. 1–6). The dreamer in the Prologue to *The Legend of Good Women* is referred to as the author of works otherwise known to be by Chaucer (F329ff., 417ff., G255ff., 344ff., 405ff.).

[3] In *Li Romanz de la Poire* Messire Thibaut embodies an acrostic of his name (ed. F. Stehlich, Halle, 1881, ll. 2413ff. and cp. ll. 2390–94); in *Le Dit de la Panthère* de Margival's name is conveyed by anagram (ll. 2630ff.); in *Vox Clamantis* the dreamer identifies himself as Gower by a syllabic cryptogram (p. 54, n. 11, above). Compare de Deguileville's acrostics in *Le Pèlerinage de la Vie Humaine* (Lydgate's translation, ii, pp. 621ff.), *Le Pèlerinage de l'Ame* (ll. 10751ff.), and *Le Pelerinage Jhesucrist* (ed. Stürzinger, London, 1897, ll. 3679ff.).

[4] As in Rutebeuf's *Voie de Paradis* (*Oeuvres*, i, ll. 18, 26–28, 307); in Raoul de Houdan's *Songe d'Enfer* (Raoul de Houdenc, *Le Songe d'Enfer*, in A. Scheler, ed., *Trouvères Belges* (*Nouvelle Série*), ii, Louvain, 1879, ll. 672, 677); in Jean de la Mote's *Voie d'Enfer et de Paradis* (*La Voie d'Enfer et de Paradis,* ed. Sister M. Aquiline Pety, Washington, 1940, ll. 4617–18); in Jean de Condé's *La Messe des Oisiaus et li Plais des Chanonesses et des Grises Nonains* (*Dits et Contes de Baudouin de Condé et de son Fils Jean de Condé*, ed. A. Scheler, iii, Brussels, 1867, ll. 1495–6); in his *Dis d'Entendement* (op. cit., l. 1497); and in Watriquet de Couvin's *Li Mireoirs as Dames* (*Dits*, ed. Scheler, l. 491).

[5] Rutebeuf, *Le Dit d'Hypocrisie*, *Oeuvres*, i, ll. 42–45.

[6] As in Rutebeuf, op. cit., l. 47, or in Houdan's *Songe d'Enfer* (ll. 411–12) or in Chaucer's *House of Fame* (l. 729). Chambers cites these instances.

[7] Deschamps, *Le Lay Amoureux*, *Oeuvres*, ii, 1880, ll. 295–6.

dreamer is, expressly or by the name conferred on him, a writer.

There are nameless dreamers in anonymous dream-vision poems, and in dream-vision poems of known authorship. These do not affect the issue, since it is no part of identifying a convention to establish that it was invariably followed. If there exists a substantive fourteenth-century poem of known authorship recounting a dream vision in the first person where the dreamer bears another name than the poet's that will be material evidence; I have failed to find one. What has been shown, I believe, is that thirteenth- and fourteenth-century French and English authors, writing various kinds of narrative poems in which a first-person narrator recounts a succession of fantastic incidents represented as experienced either awake or in a dream, would conventionally identify the narrators with themselves. Such identification was obviously not intended to be complete. At the same time it was necessarily deliberate. And whatever other functions it may have served in establishing a relationship with reader or hearer, and challenging his sense of irony, reality and truth, it had an unmistakable first purpose: to publish the author's name.

The poets who claimed authorship by this means made no difficulty over assigning to the personages named after themselves experiences necessarily fictitious because impossible in the actual world. They created the ambiguous situation where encouragement to identify poet and narrator is given by their possession of the same name and checked by the character of what is narrated; that they did this suggests that the ambiguity had a purpose. To speculate about this purpose is not part of the present discussion; to recognize the ambiguity is material. For it implies that in any argument about the authorship of *Piers Plowman* to maintain that the dreamer cannot be named after the poet because experiences which he ascribes to himself could not be biographically true is historically unaccept-able.

There would, then, seem to be very strong *a priori* grounds for believing that the Dreamer Will of the three versions of *Piers Plowman* bears the name of their author.[1] And if no fourteenth-century dream-vision poem exists in which the dreamer who recounts

---

[1] As Chambers maintained ('Robert or William', pp. 444, 450).

the vision is a total fiction with another name than the author who brought him into being, then to maintain that the Will of *Piers Plowman* is such a fiction is to posit a very remarkable exception. Exceptions can never be ruled out. But the greater likelihood is that the concept of the wholly fictitious first-person narrator in a four-teenth-century poem is anachronistic.[1]

It remains to examine the occurrences of the name Will critically, that is with respect to their disposition and function, and the activities imputed to the personage so named. In that examination considerations of autobiography have no place.[2] The names are to be viewed as parts of the text and elements in its meaning. As conventional signatures they should presumably reflect some plan or system of revealing the poet's identity, since if it seemed to him worthwhile to reveal this he is unlikely to have done so haphazardly. As elements of meaning they ought to possess at least some depth of reference. The naming of the Dreamer in *Piers Plowman* has always hitherto seemed a problem of evidence, but that may not have been its only rewarding aspect. After the establishment of the authority of the ascription in the Trinity College, Dublin manu-script and the demonstration of a fourteenth-century convention of signature the names may be otherwise approached. As an element of meaning each should reflect the poet's attitude to his subject; as part of a system of unfolding identity it ought to reveal his attitude to his reader or hearer. In those terms the successive occurrences of the name Will in the three versions will now be examined.

In the **A** version the name occurs three times: at V 43-44,

repentaunce . . . made wil to wepe watir wiþ his eiȝen;

at VIII 42-44,

marchauntis . . . ȝaf wille for his writyng wollene cloþis;
For he co[pie]de þus here clause þei [couden] hym gret mede;

---

[1] Chambers made this point ('Robert or William', pp. 442, 450-1). I hope that I have sufficiently shown my obligation to his last article. It represents the first serious study of the problem of authorship in terms of literary history.

[2] Since by the nature of the fourteenth-century convention of signature the degree of identity shared by a poet and his dreamer-namesake will be neither constant nor frequently determinable; the dreamer must always be essentially a fiction.

and at IX 61, 62, 116–18,

> A muchel man . . .
> Com ⁊ callide me be my kynde name. . . .
> þanne þou3t . . . seide þis wordis:
> 'Where þat dowel, ⁊ dobet, ⁊ dobest beþ in londe,
> Here is wil wolde wyte.'

The first occurrence introduces into a narrative situation where the personages are allegorical (Conscience and St Truth) or obviously typical (Pernel, Thomas, Wat), or actual (king, council and clergy) someone whose attributes are a name and a physical expression of contrition. This is the earliest version of the poem; factors in the poet's conception of his subject are, therefore, that his connexion with the poem (and his name) are not established; that the dreamer is still nameless and featureless; and that the reader or hearer can know only what has been told him so far line by line. Thus one designed effect of introducing this personage must be to create puzzled interest: who is he and why does he come abruptly into the story? He can shed tears; is he flesh and blood? Or is he a personification of Wilfulness, Self-Will (*NED* s.v. *Will* sb.[1] 9)? The ambiguity offers the reader a choice between an unsatisfactory literal meaning, that an unidentified actual person called Will leads the penitents, and an allegorical one, that for wilfulness to experience and be corrected by contrition is the first step towards spiritual regeneration.

Because Will has now been introduced the poet's attitude to naming him the second time must be different. It is no longer a matter of connecting him with the development but of extending the connexion. Will is said to have received tangible gifts 'for his writing' and handsome reward from the merchants 'because he copied[1] their clause'. This time the intention is evidently to represent Will as an actual person. Moreover he now appears important, no incidental participant in the action but involved in a major way, since whatever it was that he did for the merchants, this constitutes a main element of the sense. Again he has been abruptly introduced; this is to generate questions. Who is he? In what capacity did he write and copy? Do the writing and copying refer to the

---

[1] If the variant *coupide* were preferred my argument would be somewhat affected, but not, I think, materially. For the choice of *copiede* see my A text, p. 450.

same thing? The first, literal sense might seem to be that he is Truth's scribe, who actually penned the letter sealed with Truth's privy seal. But such work would be paid for by Truth, not the merchants. Will cannot have composed the merchants' pardon, which originates with God. Nevertheless he has merited joyous and open-handed reward. Then what is his connexion with the Dreamer, who refers to him in the third person? The Dreamer, reporting the contents of the sealed letter, exhibits knowledge which in the literal narrative he should not yet possess, but which Will by his writing and copying would have acquired. By this narrative illogicality the Dreamer, as the knowledgeable first-person narrator, is equated with an also knowledgeable, apparently actual person named Will, who has been rewarded by a class of actual men for writing and copying.

To the contemporary reader acquainted with the practice of signature the person Will who writes, who shares knowledge with the Dreamer, who has previously by his contrition associated him-self with sinful man, must have been the poet. For it is the poet who, in one sense, wrote the merchants' clause by giving particular expression to the general principles of morality and charity ex-pressed in it, and in another sense only copied it, since these principles which it embodies did not originate with him.

If I have read correctly, while the poet has so far revealed himself twice, briefly, as somehow involved in the action, he has not shown the extent of his involvement. This is to be made clear on the third occasion, when the connexion between him and the Dreamer hitherto only implied by the latter's use of the first person and possession of special knowledge becomes explicit. So far the Dreamer has had only the individuality of the reporting voice. Now Thought addresses him by his *kynde*, that is 'proper', 'appropriate', 'rightful' (*NED* s.v. *Kind* a. 1c, 2a), therefore also correct name; this turns out, after some delay, to be that of the writer who was re-warded. It is not conceivable that the poet can have expected his reader to view this identity of names as a coincidence; the implica-tion must be of a shared identity. The secret is out: the reader-for-the-first-time has become an informed reader. Meanwhile by the earlier references to Will in the third person the reader has received a caution against complete identification. If he is perceptive and has some knowledge of dream poetry he will have recognized both that the relationship between poet and Dreamer is conventional and that it is complex.

This lengthy process of signature reflects the state of mind of the poet. Developing, presumably for the first time, a type of identity new in his creative experience, a dramatic personality which bears his name and moves, as the dreamers of other visions have moved, back and forth across the frontiers of possible actuality, he has been sensible of diffidence, aware of imperfection, anxious to avoid arrogance in laying down the moral law. The consequence for the reader has been a process of revelation indirect and prolonged. But the convention has been observed and signature achieved. The Dreamer's name is Will, and Will is a writer.

In the **B** version the name again appears three times, at V 61–62 corresponding to **A** V 43–44; at VIII 70, 71, 122–4, corresponding to **A** IX 61, 62, 116–18, and at XV 148 where the Dreamer says

I haue lyued in londe . . . my name is longe wille.

The second occurrence of **A** (VIII 42–44) has disappeared through revision.

An important element in the poet's attitude to his subject and readers during the composition of this part of **B** must be that **B** is a revision. In the poet's mind the game of progressively revealing the nominal identity of dreamer and signatory has been played out. Thus the passage in **A** (VIII 42–44) embodying the challenge to associate Dreamer and writer gives place through revision to a reference to Piers Plowman. In another respect also the poet has advanced. Whilst he maintains the attitude of sinful humility adopted in **A** (**B** V 61–62), indeed even emphasizes it (**B** V 186–7), he now has confidence in his imaginative conception of the Dreamer; the latter's essentially ironic character as a dramatic personage has been formed, the lines of his behaviour have been laid.[1] The innovator's excitement and hesitations have given place, if the substitution at **B** VII 38 is any indication, to a new pre-occupation, with Piers and his rôle in the forthcoming development.

The third occurrence of the name Will in **B** is a quite positive

---

[1] The Dreamer is already in **A** IX–XI a more fully realized figure than in the earlier part of that version.

affirmation. Whatever the further meaning of the line,[1] it puts the Dreamer's baptismal name beyond question. By the time, moreover, that this affirmation is made the poet has unmistakably expressed his conception of the Dreamer as a writer. For at XII 16 Imagynatif has rebuked him,

þow medlest þe with makynges and myȝtest go sey þi sauter;

and the Dreamer, in proffering his excuse, has accepted the imputation:

catoun conforted his sone þat, clerke þough he were,
To solacen hym sum tyme as I do whan I make.

Whether these lines reflect the poet's own self-examination[2] is not material to this assessment. What matters is the representation of Will as a poet; and this is made twice more: at XIX 1,

Thus I awaked & wrote what I had dremed;

and at XIX 478,

I awakned þerewith & wrote as me mette.

By such insistence the poet seems intent to lessen the distinctiveness of Dreamer and writer suggested in **A** by their unspecified connexion and the third person reference to Will at **A** VIII 42–44. He will have perceived that the disappearance of the distinction can only be apparent, for just as the vision is a fiction so the waking-and-writing can at best be a figure of speech. But the poetry exists, and the actual poet has made the Dreamer lay claim to it; he has thus deliberately associated himself with the personage of his creation who bears his name, and in terms of the convention signed his poem.

In the **C** version there are also three occurrences of the name. Only one of these, however, corresponds to any in **A** or **B**: Will's contrition still introduces the confession of the Sins (VII 1–2).[3] But whereas in **A** and **B** this act of penitence was Will's first

---

[1] Discussed below, p. 67.
[2] So Chambers, Preface to Bright, *New Light*, pp. 17–18, and 'Robert or William', pp. 457–8.
[3] References are to Skeat's *C Text*.

appearance, in **C** the poet has already shown that the Dreamer is called Will at II 3–5:

> A loueliche lady . . . calde me by name
> And seide, 'wille,[1] slepest þow?'

The third occurrence of the name is still, as in **AB**, in the dialogue with Thought, but this time at the beginning (XI 68–71):

> A muche man . . .
> Cam and callede me by my kynde name.
> 'What art þow' quaþ ich, 'þat my name knowest?'
> 'That wost þou, wille',[2] quaþ he.

These changes, which abolish all delay over naming the Dreamer, reflect two new circumstances in the revising poet's attitude to his subject and audience.

The first originates in the fact that **C** is the second revision: since the completion of **B** the Dreamer has had a substantive existence; his name, nature and characteristic activities are established and published. For the poet he is now no longer the subject of the same kind of creative excitement as previously. Signature, that is the naming of the Dreamer, becomes thus in one sense a matter of convenience, to be dealt with at the first appropriate point, without elaboration, almost as a matter of form.

The second circumstance has to do with a reorganization which modifies the tone of the whole poem. It is part of another change in **C** affecting signature: the transference of the point at which the Dreamer is first represented as a writer. Such representation is again made three times in **C**; the second and the third occasions are those of **B** (**C** XXII 1 and XXII 483). But the first occurs much earlier

---

[1] There are material variants: *wille*] *why* DV (*hy* over erasure, (?) main hand V); *sone* IOLB. But the originality of *wille* is not in doubt. The variant *why* as a reflex of *wille* supports that reading. And since OLB are a genetic group support for *sone* is limited to two witnesses; their coincident variation to *sone* is doubly explicable, by memorial contamination from **A** or **B** and by alliterative inducement.

[2] There is variation: *wille*] *wel* DEQZKN. But again the originality of *wille* is practically certain. The distribution of support for *wel* requires assumption of at least four independent substitutions, but these are easy to assume on the inducement of the common collocation *witen wel*, or of memorial contamination from **A** or **B**. Confirmation of the originality of *wille* in **C** is afforded by the absence of any *wel*] *wille* variation in the corresponding **AB** passages; that *wille* here originated in revision is evident from **C** XI 124 where with one exception which is not material the manuscripts read *Her is on wolde* (v.l. *wille*) *wite* for **AB**'s *Here is wil wolde*.

than the first in **B**, before the confession of the Sins, at VI 1–5:

> ich wonede on cornehulle . . . lytel ylete by . . .
> Among lollares of london and lewede heremytes
> For ich made of[1] þo men as reson me tauhte.

The whole passage containing these lines is new, a major revision representing the Dreamer in a mood of self-critical intro-spection. Its function corresponds roughly to that of **B** XII 4–29 (not taken over into **C**),[2] and it constitutes a change in the presenta-tion rather than in the conception of the Dreamer. The reason for the change appears from the difference in the position and con-tent of the passages. That of **B**, coming relatively late in the poem as the outlines of the Dreamer's character take increasingly clear shape in the poet's imagination, represents his moral position only generally, and is concerned mainly with the rightness of his pre-occupation with verse-making. Imagynatif's rebuke does not seem to strike home; the Dreamer appears to make his point, and the impression is of his persistent versifying being if not justified at least condoned. By contrast the new **C** passage is powerfully condemna-tory: the Dreamer by his own admission emerges guilty of pride, sloth, gluttony, anger, envy, self-will and presuming on God's grace. The reasons for his tears at VII 1, 2 are abundantly prepared. Aspects of his represented personality which in **B** emerged only gradually seem here gathered together. That personality, thus early established, is a determinant of the tone and meaning of the remainder, that is the bulk of the poem: the search for sanctity and its attendant condemnations of evil are to be seen as carried out in humility; the offences of the searcher and censor are made to appear as great as any in the moral wilderness where he moves; he represents

---

[1] Notwithstanding the fact that one scribe has substituted *rouȝte* for *made* there seems no real doubt that *ich made of* here means 'I composed verses about'. To be sure the expression *maken of* is lexically ambiguous. And I appreciate that Sisam and Tolkien have translated *ich made of* respectively 'I judged' and 'I summed up' (K. Sisam, *Fourteenth Century Verse & Prose*, Oxford, 1921, p. 233 and Glossary s.v. *Make(n)*, *Mak* v.). But I cannot accept that Sisam's reason, 'Skeat's interpretation—that *made of* means 'made verses about'—is forced', has any lexical basis. *NED*'s examples for *Make* v.[1] 5b, 'to compose verses; to write poetry', are at least as good as those for 21b, 'to esteem (well or ill)'. Also the poet does not elsewhere use *maken* in the latter sense, but often uses it in the former, as e.g. in the lines quoted on p. 62 above.

[2] Cp. Donaldson, *Piers Plowman: The C-Text and Its Poet*, pp. 224–6.

himself as a moral failure whose best hope is for a divine grace that he knows he does not merit.

It was earlier demonstrated that in view of the existence of a fourteenth-century convention by which authors of dream-vision poems signed these by naming the dreamers after themselves there is every presumption that the author of the three *Piers Plowman* poems was called William. If I have correctly examined the successive occurrences of his name it should be further apparent that the Dreamer Will represents an aspect of the author's developing conception of his own work. The presence of three signatures in each version implies a systematic claim to authorship. A feature of that claim is the representation of the Dreamer as a writer, once by implication in the unfinished **A** version, three times expressly in **B** and in **C**. By naming the Dreamer after himself the author has also suggested his own involvement: imaginatively, as would be presumable, by the deliberate care devoted to the occasions of naming; but also spiritually and emotionally as appears from the revision of **C** discussed above, where he takes pains to define the moral position of the personage who serves as his voice. A probability that the poet was also biographically involved appears from the practice of other authors of allegorical narratives and dream visions. The extent of such involvement is not our concern; but it is relevant that their practice was to invite biographical association of dreamer and poet, and that this invitation is also a feature of *Piers Plowman*. From all its aspects the procedure of naming Will in *Piers Plowman* indicates that the poet was not merely publishing his own baptismal name but also implying that the Dreamer was—to some indeterminable extent—made in his own image.

One last consideration remains: has the author deliberately recorded by signature more than merely his nickname and baptismal name? This is, of course, raised by **B** XV 148, *I haue lyued in londe . . . my name is longe wille.* The line, which in the first instance completes the threefold naming of Will in **B**, is otherwise exceptional: as a particularly direct and emphatic assertion of the Dreamer's name; as a fuller identification, giving Will a nickname; and because if read as a cryptogram it surrenders the complete name *wille longelonde*, that of the author of *Piers Plowman* according to the Trinity College, Dublin ascription. The question is whether this last feature is an accident or whether the line was designed to be a full signature. For a number of reasons the latter appears to be the case.

First, experience suggests that an accident of this kind is intrinsically improbable. An ordinary man whose name lends itself to punning is likely to become intensely aware of this simply through social encounter early in life, and to notice, almost invariably, the occurrence of its homonyms. *A fortiori* it seems unlikely that a poet with such a name, himself addicted to word-play, should have written a line designed to contain his baptismal name and nickname and inadvertently have embodied in that line two words which make up his surname.

If, notwithstanding this improbability, William Langland wrote such a line at XV 148, we might fairly expect its meaning to be of main importance to the progression of the work. For if this were the case its content might have preoccupied him so wholly that he failed to notice how, while making his Dreamer emphatically specify his nickname and baptismal name, he was also recording the components of his own actual surname. But it has not been shown that XV 148 has such a character, or indeed that it has much sense of any kind beyond the ostensible meaning of its words. Attempts to interpret the line, from Manly to Fowler, have been singularly unsuccessful.[1] Other lines where the baptismal signature Will occurred arose naturally out of the larger sense and promoted this; for example when Will was named during the approach of Thought to Wit on his behalf this signified the Dreamer's rejection of the friars' glib doctrine and his turning to his own intellectual resources. I cannot see that XV 148 has any similar contextual aptness.

The context where it occurs creates an expectation that the

---

[1] Manly's proposal that it is a fourteenth-century equivalent of the archaic Americanism 'I'm from Missouri, you'll have to show me', finds no support in Middle English usage; his alternative suggestion, that *longe wille* is not a real name but 'a popular locution implying *long* experience and observation' ('The Authorship', pp. 15–16) is open to the same criticism. Fowler's notion that by the line the Dreamer asserts his conquest of self-will, his acquisition of the virtue of patience, and his capacity for long-suffering (*Literary Relations*, p. 111) is highly imaginative, but correspondingly remote from the words of the text and unapt to the context. For other discussions see Moore, 'Studies' II, pp. 28–29; Cargill, pp. 41–42; and Chambers, 'Robert or William', pp. 457, 462.

Dreamer will answer something like 'Even though I have lived to a considerable age and observed widely I have never found an instance of fulfilled charity'. If that is all the meaning of the line it is strikingly inefficient and would read better *I haue lyued longe in londe, my name is wille* (this alliterative pattern is one of the poet's), but better still without the name which, lacking immediate point, seems gratuitously inserted. Or, supposing that the line was designed to have reference in depth, then once the Dreamer invokes his own experience the allusion ought to be to preceding characterizations of him: as obsessed with his search and meanwhile no respecter of persons (XV 3–10), therefore a highly critical man; and as passionately curious (XV 47–49), therefore inferably an avid observer. If we took such allusions together with the insistence on name and nickname this might give XV 148 some meaning like 'I have lived up and down the country; I need only mention my name to invoke my reputation as an observer critical to the point of folly'. But such an interpretation seems far-fetched, and carries little conviction. Viewed as ingenuous verse the line, however one reads it, is obscure with an obscurity not characteristic of the **B** version. For its simple words no apt and necessary meaning can be found which will explain their collocation as inevitable in the manner of great poetry. The line is, moreover, tautological and thus in one sense even pointless. For by the time it occurs the reader knows the Dreamer's baptismal name and that he is represented as a tall man (VIII 70); and the Creature of Many Names whom the Dreamer addresses has nothing to learn about him (XV 13–14).

These features of the line stand out: that it is unusually emphatic for a simple signature; that unlike the other simple signatures in all versions it fails to mesh neatly, dramatically and inevitably into the structure of meaning; that it is either deeply obscure or not particularly meaningful; and that taken at its least debatable, literal sense it conveys no information which the reader and the personage addressed do not already have, except the Dreamer's nickname and a vague reference to his age.

It may of course be that at this point in the poem, which was evidently of high moment to him, the poet simply wrote an inferior line, a part of the badness of which was that it accidentally embodied the component syllables of his surname. The possibility of such an aberration, whereby he failed to notice his choice of the words which in another order made up his full name, cannot be excluded. But this possibility seems remote compared with the only alternative explanation of the line: that its form was dictated by another consideration than the advancement of the sense, an explanation which is historically authorized. For the signature of poems by this particular kind of cryptogram, which operates through punning syllabic disarrangement, was demonstrably a fourteenth-century practice. A *rondel* by Deschamps will serve to illustrate it.

> Les noms sarez du seigneur et servent
> *Cou*vertement en ce rondelet *cy*,
> Maiz diviser les vous fauldra ainsi:
>
> Une silabe prendrez premierement
> Du second ver et la fin autressy:
> Les noms sarez du seigneur et servent
> Couvertement en ce rondelet cy.
>
> En reversent prendrez subtivement
> En derrain ver troiz petiz mos de li:
> *A ce eust* bien un autre defailli.
> Les noms sarez du seigneur et servent
> Couvertement en ce rondelet cy,
> Mais diviser les vous fauldra ainsi.[1]

It is, moreover, an evident feature of texts where such crypto-grammatic signature occurs that the shaping of the puzzle over-rode other, more properly artistic considerations. The essence of Deschamps's *rondel* is the technical ingenuity applied to compliment Coucy by covertly naming patron and poet together in an exacting lyrical form. The poem has, in effect, no other meaning. By the same token if *Piers Plowman* **B** XV 148 was primarily designed to embody the poet's full name by punning syllabic disarrangement, then its apparent obscurity or deficiency of meaning is accounted for. The alternative explanation of the line requires difficult

---

[1] *Oeuvres*, iv, p. 114. *Coucy* (l. 2) is the title of a patron. A *balade* with a similar but more extended cryptogram is found at *Oeuvres*, iii, p. 381. Chambers ('Robert or William', p. 462) had cited Gower's elaborate signature of *Vox Clamantis*. The practice continued in the fifteenth century: see Jusserand's instance from Christine de Pisan (*L'Epopée Mystique*, p. 63).

assumptions of aberration and accident in an improbable combina׳ tion, and is therefore the less tenable.

A common feature of these signatures is their obscurity. In respect of this Deschamps's poem and **B** XV 148 differ less than might at first appear. The *rondel* quoted states plainly that it con׳ tains the names of lord and servant and then directs how these are to be found. The modern reader, guided by an editorial rubric and italics, like his fourteenth׳century predecessor who already knew the authorship of the poem and the patron's identity, accomplishes this without difficulty. But without such aids the instructions are not wholly clear. For one thing *premierement* in the first line of the second stanza is ambiguous, and might refer to either the action of *prendrez* or the position of the *silabe*. For another the *troiz petiz mos* are not precisely specified; the line where *A ce eust* occurs contains two others just as *petiz*. It is necessary to imagine the situation of the mediaeval reader totally ignorant of the poem's author, or how the modern reader would solve the puzzle without knowledge of the poet's identity and biography, and in the absence of an exten׳ sive body of verse confidently ascribable to Deschamps. The key to this cryptogram can never have worked perfectly except for those who knew what to look for: the names of a known author and his known patron, that is, at the time the poem was written, for a coterie.[1]

Similarly the signature of XV 148 is not wholly open. Although the line is apparently keyed by the words *my name is* its full hidden meaning would be denied, it must seem, to anyone initially ignorant of the poet's surname. Readers of his time who knew this were equipped to value the line at full. Those who did not would certainly be made to notice the baptismal name; they might also interpret the insistent tone, the expression *I haue lyued in londe*, and the graphic detail of the nickname, as confirmation that Will was the name of the actual poet.[2] There is no ground for believing that,

---

[1] Deschamps's other poem, the *balade* referred to above (p. 68, n. 1), is even more obscure. It professes to contain the names of the poet and a mistress, but offers no aids. Presumably, then, it was in the first instance open only to the mistress. The poem is generally very difficult in consequence of the dominance of the sense by the cryptogram.

[2] So much and no more can be inferred from the *nota*'s in various manuscripts at this point, as will be evident. In Trinity College, Cambridge MS B.15.17 the name and nickname only are ruled round; in the Newnham College Yates Thompson MS they are omitted, presumably for subsequent insertion by a rubricator. Four copies, Oriel College MS 79,

in ignorance of the existence of a poet called Langland, they would have found that name in the line.[1]

To an objection that there would be little point for an author to conceal his name in his poem in such a fashion that it could be identified only by those who already knew him to be its poet the answer must be that such practice occurred. For the case in *Piers Plowman* there are various possible explanations: that the poet was writing, first and foremost, for a circle of readers which knew his name; that the poem was a dangerous document, not to be too openly acknowledged, but which he could not forbear to sign in his own way; that as an ironist he derived satisfaction and pleasure from this unrevealing revelation. These explanations, while only speculative, are not without weight. Taking all considerations into account there is much probability of XV 148 containing a full signature by William Langland, and no great argument for its embodying the name of the otherwise attested author by accident.

To sum up this last assessment: since the occurrences of the name Will in the *Piers Plowman* poems and the cryptogrammatic possibilities of **B** XV 148 can be tested against known facts of literary history they are potentially historical evidence of authorship. The test gives them unexpected weight. They appear as clear instances of conformity to a contemporary literary convention, in accordance with which the poet systematically lays claim to the successive versions of his dream-vision poem by naming its Dreamer-Narrator after himself, and once, to those able to identify it, reveals his full name. They concur, authoritatively, with the other information available in the present state of knowledge about the authorship of *Piers Plowman*. Their import that the name of the author of each version was William, and that the surname of the author of the **B** version was Langland, is further evidence of single authorship and must be taken seriously as such.

Cambridge University Library MS Ll.4.14, Bodley MS Rawlinson Poet.38, and B.M. Additional MS 35287 have marginal entries, *longe wille*, beside the line in fifteenth- or sixteenth-century hands. One copy, Bodley MS Laud Misc. 581, has in the margin in a sixteenth-century hand *nota the name* of *thaucto*[*ur*]; another, B.M. Additional MS 10574, reads marginally in a fifteenth-century hand *Nomen auctoris* / [*h*]*uius libri est longe wille*. None of the several distinct identifications implied by the genetic distribution of these manuscripts goes beyond name and nickname.

[1] This is a consideration which must enhance the authority of the Trinity College, Dublin ascription.

V

CONCLUSION

It is now necessary to survey the results of my assessment. These are
not contingent; the order of the assessment was prescribed by the
history of the subject, and must not imply any dependence of one
finding upon another.

First, the authority of the Trinity College, Dublin ascription of
Piers Plowman to William Langland is not, in the present state of
knowledge, subject to challenge. Its early date, the evident know-
ledgeableness of its author, the absence of historical reasons for
suspecting the information contained in it, the unlikelihood that its
poet's surname was inferred from **B** XV 148, and the dubious
quality of the conflicting ascriptions to William W. or to Robert
Langland, establish this ascription as evidence of major importance.

Second, all near-contemporary and early indications are to the
effect that the 'book which is called Piers Plowman' named in the
Trinity College, Dublin ascription was not any particular version
of the poem but the poem in any or all its forms; and these indications further imply the existence of an early tradition of the
single authorship of *Piers Plowman*.

Third, on the evidence of mediaeval conventions of signature the
name Will given to the Dreamer in all three versions was also the
name of the poet, who by so employing it signed his poem, and also,
again on the evidence of conventional practice, once embodied in
a cryptogram his full name, that of the author according to the
Trinity College, Dublin ascription.

Thus all external and historical evidence of any authority attests
that the three versions of *Piers Plowman* were written by a single man.
Obviously the force of this evidence is not overpowering; it is not
the equivalent of a sworn and reliably witnessed deposition, 'Be it
known to all future students of English Literature that I, William
Langland, wrote all three versions of the poem about man, society,
religion and God which its readers are already beginning to call

Piers Plowman'. But in default of such certainty, which would indeed be a rare legacy from the Middle Ages, the common effect of this external and historical evidence is entirely unambiguous; reasonably and correctly understood it has a single, unmistakable import. It contains no ghost of a reason for believing in the multiple authorship of *Piers Plowman*.

Meanwhile the theory of multiple authorship which generated the controversy, and which was constructed either in disregard of this evidence or in ignorance of it, appears critically unsound and logically deficient, with one of its main premises unfounded.

The question of the single or multiple authorship of *Piers Plowman* is thus not in the present state of knowledge a matter of opinion. The direction of the evidence is that the three forms of the poem are records of a single writer's successive attempts to realize an imaginative and creative experience. It follows, then, that all phenomena of their difference or similarity, whether textual or literary, are to be interpreted according to that direction.